"Although there are some differences between managing non-profit institutions and for-profit companies, a common set of unwritten rules defines decision making in the executive suite of almost any organization. Bob Frisch understands those rules, and in *Who's in the Room?* he clearly describes both why they are so pervasive and the detrimental impact they can have on your management team dynamics. More importantly, he presents a straightforward approach to making the rules of how your organization makes critical decisions more transparent and effective."
—Charles Roussel, CEO, College of American Pathologists

"CEOs—and the people who work for them—are going to be talking about *Who's in the Room?* This important new book addresses how decisions really get made. It takes the issue of top team effectiveness out of the realm of traditional team building and into questions of process and structure and required flexibility. It provides a practical guide to raising your impact as a leader."
—Gretchen W. McClain, CEO, Xylem Inc.

"*Who's in the Room?* offers executives unique insights into how executive decisions really happen. Frisch draws on his experience and shares stories of how senior leaders make decisions, use kitchen cabinets, and unleash employee energy. He also offers guidance on structures, processes, and roles for high-performing teams. The book is pragmatic and relevant for any executive who realizes that much of today's work has to be done through relationships and collaboration."
—Dave Ulrich, professor, Ross School of Business, University of Michigan; and partner, The RBL Group

"Companies, and the numerous issues that arise around decision making, are always much more complex and dynamic than the whittled-down portraits typically offered by the media and in business school cases. Here, Bob Frisch does the opposite of that. Instead of over-simplifying reality to make solutions more accessible, he provides a more sophisticated and elegant set of frameworks to directly acknowledge the complexity of organizations, and specifically how people act within them. The result is a book which is engaging, and most importantly, practical."

—Eric Korman, senior vice president, strategy and business development, Ralph Lauren Corporation

"Are you in the room when your company's important decisions are made? Do you have the right people in the room when you need advice on key decisions? Bob Frisch's deep experience and insightful analysis will help you build stronger teams and make better decisions. *Who's in the Room?* is essential reading for anyone in, or aspiring to, the senior executive suite."

—Charles Fine, professor, MIT Sloan School of Management; and author, *Clockspeed*

WHO'S
IN THE
ROOM?

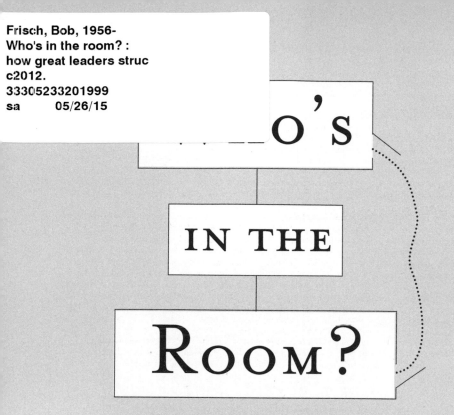

O'S

IN THE

ROOM?

How Great Leaders Structure and Manage
the Teams Around Them

BOB FRISCH

JOSSEY-BASS
A Wiley Imprint
www.josseybass.com

Published by Jossey-Bass
A Wiley Imprint
One Montgomery Street, Suite 1200, San Francisco, CA 94104-4594—www.josseybass.com

Some of the discussion in Chapter Four of executive teams as legislatures has been adapted from "Off-Sites That Work," by Bob Frisch and Logan Chandler (*Harvard Business Review*, June 2006, pp. 117–126), and "When Teams Can't Decide," by Bob Frisch (*Harvard Business Review*, November 2008, pp. 121–126).

Some of the discussion in Chapter Seven of testing walls and fences has been adapted from "When Teams Can't Decide," by Bob Frisch (*Harvard Business Review*, November 2008, pp. 121–126).

Some of the material in the extended discussion of the Marquis de Condorcet's voting paradox in Chapter Four has been reprinted with permission from "When Teams Can't Decide," by Bob Frisch (*Harvard Business Review*, November 2008, pp. 121–126). Copyright © 2008 by Harvard Business Publishing; all rights reserved.

Jossey-Bass books and products are available through most bookstores. To contact Jossey-Bass directly call our Customer Care Department within the U.S. at 800-956-7739, outside the U.S. at 317-572-3986, or fax 317-572-4002.

Wiley also publishes its books in a variety of electronic formats and by print-on-demand. Some material included with standard print versions of this book may not be included in e-books or in print-on-demand. If the version of this book that you purchased references media such as CD or DVD that was not included in your purchase, you may download this material at http://booksupport.wiley.com. For more information about Wiley products, visit www.wiley.com.

Library of Congress Cataloging-in-Publication Data

Frisch, Bob.
  Who's in the room: how great leaders structure and manage the teams around them / Bob Frisch. -1st ed.
     p. cm.
  Includes index.
   ISBN 978-1-118-06787-1 (hardback); ISBN 978-1-118-17007-6 (ebk);
ISBN 978-1-118-17008-3 (ebk); ISBN 978-1-118-17009-0 (ebk)
  1.   Decision making. 2.   Senior leadership teams. 3.   Chief executive officers.
4.   Executives. I. Title.
  HD30.23.F755 2012
  658.4′022-dc23

                                                                    2011039775

Printed in the United States of America

FIRST EDITION
HB Printing 10 9 8 7 6 5 4 3 2 1

Contents

For Iris

WHO'S
IN THE
ROOM?

Introduction

Who's in the Room?

At the heart of every organization chart lies a myth.

At the top there's the boss. Directly beneath are the boss's direct reports—anywhere from five to fifteen people who meet regularly as the senior team. Whether at the corporate, divisional, functional, or departmental level, this team almost invariably has a name that suggests its lofty status: Executive Committee, Management Council, Operating Committee, Senior Management Team. Like the gods on Olympus, the members of this august body are presumed by most managers to spend their time together discussing profound thoughts and making all of the organization's truly momentous decisions.

The reality is that they don't—any more than they wear togas and sandals.

The senior team may be consulted or informed, but the most important decisions are rarely made by a group like this sitting around a conference table. Instead, the organization's leader typically calls in an inner core of intimate advisers—a *kitchen cabinet*—along with any other individuals who might shed light on a specific situation. It is this team with no name—ad hoc, unofficial, and flexible in makeup—that is the group in the room as the actual decisions get made. Yet we all persist in believing that the senior team should be the forum for decision making.

It can be a destructive belief.

I have spent the past twenty-nine years consulting to organizations of all kinds, from Fortune 500 companies to family-held businesses to the U.S. Department of State. I've earned over eight million American Airlines AAdvantage miles facilitating strategy discussions with senior executive teams in fourteen countries on five continents. Over and over during those years I have seen the confusion and conflict caused by the way decisions get made. Executives on the senior team resent the boss's end runs. They feel shut out of the big decisions, and this leads to doubts and insecurity about their own status. Will they be consulted before the next major decision is made or only informed after? Will their opinions be solicited, and how much weight will they carry?

Meanwhile, the boss is often frustrated by the apparent parochialism of individual team members and the seeming inability of subordinates to get anything done without having the boss sitting in on every discussion. The team is said to be dysfunctional. Blame is plentiful on all sides.

But this blame is misplaced. Most of the world's best executives make decisions in ways that don't show up on an organization chart or a process flow diagram. When it comes to critical decisions, they implicitly understand the inherent limitations of the formal executive team. They tacitly acknowledge that it's desirable for the boss to have the ability to vary who is in the room when major decisions are being made. And they instinctively know exactly whom they want with them in the room for each specific decision.

My purpose here is to make explicit how leaders of management teams actually work—and why they work in these particular ways. This book is grounded in a simple truth: having a small cadre of trusted advisers in the room when each big decision is made is the way most leaders run their organizations, and when the real nature of the executive team is fully understood it will also be clear that this approach is the *best* way.

Senior teams have undeniable strengths, and they are in a unique position to do things that no other group in the organization can do as well. Making big decisions isn't one of them—for very good reasons that will be dissected here. Unless the senior team's limitations are understood and its genuine strengths put to work, the blame and frustration on all sides will continue. The organization will have the approach half right: ad hoc decision making by the few. But it will also have the approach half wrong because it will fail to fully leverage the real power and competencies of the many.

My hope is that by understanding the nature of executive decision making, executives and the members of their senior teams can stop beating up themselves and each other. They can start improving the ad hoc decision-making process that probably already lies near at hand, and they can focus the executive team on what it does best. This outcome doesn't require organizational overhauls or irrelevant team-building exercises. It requires only an acceptance of reality and a willingness to refine that reality with a few simple steps that can be taken tomorrow.

For almost three decades, I've seen company after company trying to overcome what it sees as a lack of executive team effectiveness. Days, weeks, or even months of effort are wasted with little or no result. This book is meant to help you and your executive team—and similar teams at any level of your organization—to reframe the problem, to help you to stop seeing it as an issue of individual or group behavior and to start seeing what's really happening in both your formal team meetings around the leadership table and in your meetings with your kitchen cabinet. Once you do, it's unlikely you'll look at your team in the same way ever again.

It's time to send the psychologists packing. Time to stop hamstringing yourself and selling the members of your executive team short. And time to free decision making and decision makers throughout your organization from the tyranny of the organization chart.

The organization will get faster, better decisions and a higher level of organizational alignment in executing against those decisions. Team members, and the people who work under them, will achieve new levels of effectiveness—and even fulfillment—in being unleashed to do what they do best. And you and other leaders in the organization will see a dramatic drop-off in people coming into your offices and asking, "Why wasn't I in the room?"

PART ONE

From Problem to Portfolio

CHAPTER 1

Most Companies Are Run by Teams with No Names

The chief information officer (CIO) of a major industrial company—let's call him Dave—was frustrated. He had just come from the latest meeting of the company's Senior Management Team (SMT), consisting of the CEO, the presidents of the three divisions, and functional heads like him. Twelve people in all, and in his mind the team that ran the company. But now he was no longer sure exactly *what* the team did.

In preparation for the meeting, Dave had spent his Saturday evening reviewing a two-inch binder containing the business case for a major plant expansion in China. He was no expert on manufacturing or strategy, but he did know that some other major initiatives that would require significant information technology (IT) involvement were in the pipeline for later in the year. If the China expansion went ahead in the time frame outlined in the business case, it was going to be tough to come up with sufficient resources for all the projects already approved, let alone the ones yet to come in the next few quarters. When the time came to implement the plan, conflicts would inevitably arise and would compromise several other projects and possibly the China plant expansion itself. Dave had wanted to be prepared to discuss these potential resource conflicts intelligently when the business case came up on the SMT agenda on Monday morning.

Meanwhile, the week before, the CEO had met with the chief financial officer (CFO), the heads of Strategy and Operations, and the head of the Industrial Division, which wanted the plant expansion. For several intense hours the CEO had questioned this ad hoc group about the business case, which itself had been six months in the making. He concluded that the proposed expansion fit with the company's aggressive new strategy. The division knew how to navigate the tricky operating environment in China. The financials looked good. At the end of the meeting, the CEO decided that it was a go and said that he would have it put on the agenda for the next SMT meeting.

Bright and early Monday morning the SMT duly convened. The members finished up their coffee and muffins, the lights went down, the first PowerPoint slide came on the screen, and the business case team made its pitch. When the lights came back up the CEO said to the SMT members, "So, what do you all think?"

The head of Human Resources spoke up immediately, addressing the business case presenter: "At their quarterly review, the sales force said they needed to significantly ramp up the number of China region salespeople in the second and third quarters. But we have only a handful of Mandarin-speaking HR specialists to supplement our local partners. I'm just not sure we can staff up the sales force and bring on the additional personnel we're going to need at the same time. I know we provided you with local labor costs and job skills definitions, but I don't think we've adequately covered the HR support requirements from the perspective of a major staff increase."

Before the presenter could respond, the CEO intervened. "That's a good point, Susan," he said to the HR head. "But why don't you take that off-line and work it out with Operations. Today, I want everyone to look at this initiative from a company-wide perspective, not from a functional, parochial point of view." He gazed around the conference table, looking at no one in particular. "Any other questions or comments?"

Susan fell silent. Dave, the CIO, swallowed his objections. "This train has left the station," he thought, "and only an idiot would throw himself in front of a moving train." When his turn to comment came he made some bland, complimentary remarks about the plan—as did most of the other SMT members.

Now, an hour later, he sat in his office thinking about what had just happened. Sure, some of Dave's people had contributed technical data during the development of the business case and validated some of its assumptions. But his team certainly hadn't been asked how this plant expansion would dovetail with all the other priority programs requiring significant IT involvement. That wasn't their job. Balancing resources across the overall project portfolio was Dave's job, and he felt he should have had a chance to review the trade-offs involved with his colleagues before the China plant approval came barreling down the track.

Dave knew that some of the other members of the SMT—Susan for one—felt the same way. Moreover, in his six months with the company, this was the third time a major decision had steamrollered its way through an SMT meeting. "What," Dave wondered, "is the point of having an SMT if its highest purpose seems to be rubber-stamping done deals? Why do we bother to meet if the major decisions are all getting made before we even meet, with most of us out of the loop?"

The Myth of the Top Team

The CIO had fallen prey to one of the central myths of management: that a Senior Management Team, consisting of the boss and the boss's direct reports, makes the major decisions for the organization. This myth isn't restricted to Fortune 500 companies like Dave's. It permeates almost all organizations—for-profits and nonprofits, large corporations and small enterprises.

The reality is that in most of these organizations, and at most levels of management—divisional, business unit, regional, functional, departmental—major decisions are typically made by the leader, who consults with the same handful of people, perhaps joined by a few others with special knowledge of the issue, meeting together for that specific purpose. Despite the almost universal use of these informal teams—or *kitchen cabinets*—it's the rare company, division, or other unit that shows anything at the top of its organization chart except the boss and the boss's staff, constituting some sort of Senior Management Team.

The term *kitchen cabinet* has its origins in U.S. history. It began as a term of abuse used by the political opponents of President Andrew Jackson to describe the loose collection of advisers he used, in parallel with the official cabinet (the *parlor cabinet*), to make important decisions. In nineteenth-century American dwellings the kitchen was literally a smoke-filled room that was kept hidden from guests, whereas the parlor presented the publicly acceptable face of the home. As Jackson's bitter enemy Nicholas Biddle wrote of the administration, "The kitchen predominates over the parlor." Today, of course, *kitchen cabinet* is applied to any leader's unofficial group of top advisers, but the term's contentious beginnings are worth keeping in mind.

Occasionally the top level of an organization will consist of an Office of the Chairman or Office of the CEO, with more than one member, but in the vast majority of cases—at every level of the enterprise—these very real and very critical decision-making inner circles are well known and yet invisible on the formal organization charts. Chris Callero, the president and chief operating officer (COO) of Experian, the global information company, says, "It's usually the CEO, the CFO, and I who directionally steer and shape critical decisions when necessary. We do this without formal meetings, and we don't have a name."

At Berkshire Hathaway, it's Warren Buffett and Charlie Munger. At Microsoft, it was Bill Gates and Steve Ballmer. At Disney, it was Michael Eisner and Frank Wells. At the Property and Casualty Division of CIGNA, division president Gerry Isom had a standing weekend golf game with his chief lieutenants, Bill Palgutt and Dick Wratten. It was widely believed around the watercoolers that most major decisions were made by the time Gerry, Bill, and Dick took the clubhouse turn and that they spent the back nine making plans for the week ahead.

These ex officio groups aren't convened only by CEOs. Says the leader of a major conglomerate's portfolio of commercial businesses: "I see the SMT as a forum for briefing everyone. But if there's a specific decision coming, and we want to keep pressing forward, I'll go schedule a meeting with our CEO. I always invite the CFO because our CEO is going to look for the CFO to make a financial determination. Then if the issue has to do with IT or communications or some other particular area, I'll invite [the area head] as appropriate."

All managers rely on a variety of groups at different levels to get things done—think of how many task forces, steering committees, and initiative teams exist today in your enterprise, in addition to the informal conversational groups that ebb and flow in the course of a week. Companies operate through an elaborate network of formal and informal teams, some permanent and others that may last only an hour. But if you ask most managers in most companies who has approval authority over the most important decisions, invariably they will say it's their local version of the SMT—whatever name it goes by and at whatever level of the organization such a formal team is found. It's the boss and the boss's staff—the top two levels on the organization chart.

Although the phrase *kitchen cabinet* comes from American history, the phenomenon it names isn't limited to the United States. Ajay Banga, the CEO of MasterCard, who has worked in Asia, Europe, and the United States, has seen it at many levels in a variety of cultures. When he was working in India for Nestlé the firm's managing director had an executive team of nine or ten people but made most decisions in concert with his factory manager and head of HR. "The managing director had once been factory manager, so he felt most comfortable with his current factory manager," recalls Banga. "They understood each other and the guy had worked with him for years, so there was this mutual trust society."

As president, John F. Kennedy surrounded himself with a team of people presumed to be among the best and brightest in public life, academia, and private enterprise. But his closest adviser by far was his brother Robert Kennedy. Faced with a momentous issue, JFK would certainly solicit the advice of key Cabinet members and other members of his leadership team, but when it came time to make a decision he would often confer with Bobby, alone. No one else in the administration enjoyed as much influence over virtually every area of policy.

The official White House photos taken during the Cuban missile crisis capture the two men standing, deep in conversation, with the fate of the world hanging in the balance. In his official role Bobby had no reason to be involved in the issue at all. His title was attorney general, not secretary of state or secretary of defense. But with kitchen cabinets titles don't matter—it's the trust the top leader places in the wisdom of the other people in the room. From that point of view, the attorney general's real title was "the president's brother Bobby."

It is Bobby, after all, who is widely credited with coming up with the masterstroke—ignoring Soviet leader Nikita Khrushchev's second, more belligerent cable and responding to his first, more conciliatory one—that averted nuclear war during those thirteen tense days in October 1962.

Illusion and Reality

When I was a student one of the standard questions on literature exams was to discuss "illusion and reality" in Shakespeare's *Hamlet*. We would dutifully write about the distinction between the "playacting" of the characters and what they were really doing. The same distinction could be applied to the story of the plant expansion.

At Dave's company, the illusion is that on such-and-such a date the SMT approved a plant expansion in China, a decision that the CEO then took to the board of directors. That's how it appears in the records of the SMT and the minutes of the board, and that's how it looks on the organization's process flow chart. And that's what everyone in the organization believes, except for the people who know what really happened—the CEO and the members of the SMT themselves.

Like Hamlet, they know the reality behind the illusion: the decision was actually made by the CEO, meeting with a few advisers, in the week before the SMT convened. As one executive puts it about SMT meetings in general, using another theatrical reference, "Those meetings are as fine a piece of Kabuki as you will ever see." Or as Jim Noble, senior vice president of IT & Business Services for Talisman Energy; former managing director, Global Technology, at Merrill Lynch; and former CIO at Altria, says, "The CEO looks around the table and another big decision gets nodded through."

In a series of interviews, I asked top executives to estimate how often they have seen the discussion of a business case by their leadership team result in a project being rejected or substantially altered. In the aggregate, they said that it happens far less than 10 percent of the time. Typically, I received answers like "once or twice in the past five years."

The leadership team has a purpose, but it is clearly not to pass judgment on business cases. "It's always unanimous," says Experian's Chris Callero.

Says Ellyn McColgan, former president and chief operating officer of Morgan Stanley's Global Wealth Management Group, "Once you get to the highest level, the point of the meeting is to get out of the room without saying anything controversial, without raising an issue, and certainly not asking for help. Your job is to make your three minutes of airtime positive and good and then leave. That means that decision making happens somewhere else."

At one level—the performance of the company—simply nodding through decisions can lead to problems with implementation down the road. In our example the concerns of the CIO and HR head about how the China project fits with other priorities and activities never made it to the surface. You can be sure that those concerns about resource constraints and pressures will emerge once the project is under way. When people wonder why more of a company's initiatives aren't more successful, the answer might very well go back to the very days and the very meetings in which the SMT nominally approved those initiatives.

But there is a more pervasive problem—the frustration that grows in the gap between the illusion and the reality. Members of executive teams become frustrated by the timing and quality of their involvement in major decisions. More corrosively, the gap can intensify turf wars and intramural politics, as top executives compete for the CEO's ear. Some may view the leader as an autocrat. Says a former Fortune 500 division head about his boss at the time, "Generally, only Finance and Legal were at the table with him when decisions were made. I felt disenfranchised, like my voice didn't matter, so I quit giving input."

Says a Fortune 500 CEO of his experience with a former boss and that boss's kitchen cabinet: "It was a classic case of the executive team feeling that they had no role to play in the decision-making process—and, in fact, feeling insecure, threatened, and positively apprehensive at every meeting. Every guy on the team would talk to his people, in some way, about his concerns about this dysfunction."

At the furthest extreme are those leaders who shut out their executive teams altogether. The chairman and CEO of a major international bank included in his kitchen cabinet his vice chairman, his CFO, and two outside consultants widely resented by other members of the SMT. Says one insider from that time: "He would bounce things off the members of that inner circle, and there was otherwise a revolving door on his executive team, with people constantly coming and going. As a result, his immediate management team was a bunch of empty, interchangeable suits. And it created a lack of management depth at the bank, which was very apparent, very quickly, at the senior-most levels. He would just reshuffle the deck every time he got tired of a guy's face, because he only cared about those two external consultants and the two insiders. Everyone else was expendable."

Whether used wisely or poorly, kitchen cabinets are an ineradicable fact of organizational life. Their use is almost universal. Virtually every CEO I interviewed for this book and almost every CEO I've worked with—including some of the world's best—depend on a small group of trusted advisers that they consult about most major decisions. As the executive ultimately accountable to the board, the CEO has every right to consult anyone he or she pleases in making a major decision. Even a CEO who believes that the spread of kitchen cabinet management throughout his company was responsible for some of its troubles in the past finds himself being drawn back into it. "I think it just creates enormous bad behavior," he says. "But we've gone back and forth—from a kitchen cabinet with a couple of internal and external people to an executive team of fifteen to eighteen people meeting together and no kitchen cabinet; and now back to a smaller executive team of eight or ten and a kitchen cabinet."

The fact is that a kitchen cabinet offers advantages that almost no leader is willing to give up:

- It enables the CEO to consult with precisely the right mix of advisers for a particular decision.

- Because it is a small, highly selective group, it preempts the problems of endless discussion, uneven qualifications, and competition over turf that plague larger, more representative teams.

- It frees the CEO from the organization chart, which describes reporting relationships, not decision processes or decision

rights. Involving all of the CEO's direct reports in every decision is inefficient.

- It provides the CEO with the candor and the confidentiality that only a small, highly trusted group can provide and
that is critical in making major decisions with far-reaching
implications for the company internally and externally.

These unofficial, ad hoc groups are a powerful asset, and so
leaders have employed them since the dawn of recorded history.
Leaders are not only unlikely to give up kitchen cabinets, they
shouldn't give them up. Ultimately, the issue is not whether the
kitchen cabinet has supplanted the SMT or usurped its role, but
how best to use *each* team.

The Problem That Isn't There, But Won't Go Away

The next time Dave sat down with the CEO, he was careful not to
bring up his "parochial" reservations about the China project, and
he was extremely reluctant to register his real concern about the
SMT. Nevertheless, as diplomatically as possible, he suggested
to the CEO that the SMT should have been more involved
in the decision or at least brought into the decision-making
process earlier.

Dave's reluctance is understandable. Like most executives, he
knew the unwritten rules of behavior and the expectations of
bosses: *Bring me solutions, not problems. No surprises. Once a decision has been made, everyone needs to get on the bus.* Dave didn't
want to come across as petulant, a whiner. Nobody does.

It is precisely this reluctance to raise the problem that makes
it so hard to address—or even see. I have listened to scores of
executives express privately the kind of frustration that Dave felt
and then, in the next breath, dismiss the problem with "that's
the way it is."

One boss who has thought long and hard about the problem
is the CEO of a global industrial company. "My CFO, my head

of Strategy and Business Development, and I sit in my office and make decisions, and then we bring them to the Senior Management Team," he says. "The members of the team say, 'Wait a minute, did our vote count or not, did our decision matter or not?' That's up in the air right now. But I have asked whether we want to have the strategic discussion up front at the meeting in respect to our portfolio of businesses. For now, I've decided that it is something we should discuss as an SMT, though any decision is ultimately mine."

Many CEOs, however, remain unaware of their executives' frustration when it comes to this issue. From their position at the top of the pyramid they see only the smiling faces of satisfied subordinates looking up at them. And the members of the group who could broach the subject with the CEO—those who have his utmost trust and whose candor he appreciates—are most often members of the kitchen cabinet and so have no reason to disrupt the status quo.

On the rare occasions when CEOs do hear the rumblings, they might reply much as Dave's boss did to Dave's low-key protest:

First, it's absolutely normal for me to review a business case with the proposing executive and have my CFO there to highlight financial issues. They're reviewing it with *me*. I can't have twelve people in the room every time I review a document. I bring in the people who need to be there on a situational basis.

Second, we brought it to the SMT and there was an opportunity for people to raise concerns. Susan brought something up, but it wasn't a go/no-go objection—it sounded pretty operational. And when I asked what everyone thought they said it looked good or they said nothing. Nobody, including you, said, "We've got to rethink this."

What this CEO didn't say was that in the final analysis he didn't have to review anything with any of his subordinates—his authority and accountability lay with the board. He certainly wasn't obligated to seek the approval of the SMT, but he had done it anyway. What Dave didn't say was that in his mind he hadn't approved anything—unless you define approval as waving at a speeding train as it races by.

Dave's meeting with the CEO ended inconclusively, and things went on much as before. The CEO, seeing the SMT as unwieldy and inefficient, continued to consult with ad hoc teams when he was mulling over big decisions. Dave continued to chafe in his ill-defined role as a member of the SMT, but he never again raised the subject with the boss. And he cut down the number of weekend hours he spent reviewing two-inch-thick business case binders—from then on, a quick skim through the material for glaring errors was enough for him.

Two rational people, two rational positions. The CIO, as a member of the SMT, understandably thinks he and his peers should be included in major decisions. After all, the charter of this company's SMT says that it will be "the senior decision-making body of the corporation." The leader, as CEO, understandably wants the freedom and flexibility to make major decisions when and with whom he thinks best—power that the governance structure of the corporation gives him anyway. Both are playing the game by the rules that most corporations operate under.

But the game can be costly. The company's highest-paid and most valuable executives waste their time in meetings discussing foregone conclusions. Dissatisfaction with decisions simmers just beneath the surface and metastasizes to other executive teams as those decisions cascade downward. Feelings of disempowerment are pervasive. And even though team members may like and respect each other and feel pride in being part of the leadership group, they feel that this group lacks a clear sense of purpose.

The CFO of one Fortune 500 corporation put his finger directly on the problem: "Role clarity in most organizations is very weak," he told me. "Organizations give people titles, form groups, and then make decisions around the groups. And it causes confusion."

Yet the problem may not be apparent to everyone. Fred Adair and Richard Rosen conducted a study a few years ago, for the global executive search firm Heidrick & Struggles, on top-management team performance.[1] They surveyed 124 CEOs worldwide and 579 of those CEOs' reports. One of the survey questions asked respondents to rate whether leadership team decision processes were clear. On a 1 to 7 scale, with 7 being the best score, the CEOs rated this process clarity, on average, at 5.62. The executives who worked for them returned a rating of only 3.86.

In general the study showed that the CEOs surveyed had a much more positive view of the performance of their teams than their executives did. Only 28 percent of the CEOs said that they have problems with their teams, and on average they rated overall team effectiveness at 5.39 on the 1 to 7 scale. Team members rated overall effectiveness at only 4.02, and 52 percent of them said that their teams lack effectiveness in areas like leading change, driving innovation, and working cross-functionally to increase revenue.

In the face of such evidence, I would ask just one question of those leaders who aren't hearing complaints from their executive teams, who would deny that there's a problem, or who would shrug off any such problem as an unavoidable fact of corporate life: Why are so many companies expending so much effort trying to fix their leadership teams?

Note

1. Rich Rosen and Fred Adair, *How CEOs and Top Management Team Members* Really *See Their Performance* (Chicago: Heidrick & Struggles International Inc., 2008). Internal document. Used by permission.

CHAPTER 2

Team Building Won't Solve the Problem

Despite the fact that CEOs didn't indicate on the Heidrick & Struggles survey that their Senior Management Teams (SMTs) are broken, there is a constant pressure to somehow fix the current situation. The status quo seems unacceptable. It's a rare strategy offsite or management retreat that doesn't include at least one agenda item facilitated by a coach, trainer, psychologist, or organizational consultant. At the time this chapter was being written, a Google search for the phrase *leadership team development* returned 9,430,000 hits. An entire industry exists with the sole purpose of improving team effectiveness.

CEOs may show confidence in their teams when they fill out consultants' surveys, but actions speak louder than words. The corporate emphasis on team-building activities implies that the problem lies with the team itself—somehow the SMT isn't working to its potential—and that the root cause is psychological. To quote Pogo, the long-ago comic strip character:

"We have met the enemy and he is us." If the problem weren't psychological, why would we have spent the last several decades bringing in specialists to help senior management behave differently? Whether the focus is "fierce conversations" or "crucial conversations" or "trust" or "straight talk" or any of the other buzzwords that surround team-building efforts, these sessions work on improving how SMT members interact with each other.

Maybe the real story behind the discontent felt by our CIO Dave isn't that key decisions are made when he isn't in the room. Perhaps it's that members of the Senior Management Team, including Dave, are suffering from some fundamental failings of human nature that poison group dynamics. No wonder the group can't seem to make decisions, work together smoothly, or use its time together efficiently.

> *Diagnosis.* The team must be dysfunctional.
>
> *Treatment.* Bring on the team-building exercises, the ropes courses, the inspirational speakers, the communications workshops, the role-playing sessions on giving and receiving feedback. We have nothing to lose but the chains of our disaffection and everything to gain in a massive upgrade of team effectiveness.

There are only two things wrong with this picture: the diagnosis is wrong, and the treatment isn't going to solve the problem.

Let me be clear. An executive coach can perform a valuable service. At one time or another, almost everyone has had the experience of working with someone who is difficult. Such people may be arrogant, abrasive, or overbearing. They may be devious. They may pursue their self-interest at all costs, fail to deliver on promises, or shirk their responsibilities. Their bad behavior irks colleagues and can be highly disruptive on any team.

Confronted with such a character, a perceptive boss may call in a coach who can help to change deeply ingrained habits, smooth the rough edges, and generally reform the offender. In less dire cases, where some kinks in the individual's working style are getting in the way of results or an aspect of an executive's capability needs improvement, a good coach can help that executive achieve better performance in the job.

But when the focus is team building with the SMT, it's another story. Team members may feel better after one of these sessions and like or understand each other more. But from a decision-making perspective, or in terms of the SMT's becoming more effective in its role of leading the organization, these exercises are largely ineffective and beside the point. Further, the philosophical and empirical foundations of team building are shaky. Its stated goal of *team effectiveness* is so general and unmeasurable as to be almost meaningless. Most important, the problem team building is typically being applied against isn't psychological or behavioral at all.

When the Shrinks Go Marching In

If you work long enough in an organization of any size or just spend any weekday walking through a business hotel or conference center, sooner or later you will encounter a team-building exercise. In my experience with guiding strategy offsites I've seen plenty. The exercise can be as simple as seeing how tall a tower the team can build with a ream of ordinary office paper in a limited amount of time (requiring participants to collaborate, sort through ideas quickly, and execute). It can be as uncomfortable as publicly discussing 360-degree-feedback survey results about each team member. Or it can be as elaborate as flying the management team to Aspen for a few days of rafting down the Colorado River. What do team members get from such activities? They may feel a heightened sense of camaraderie. They may be able to talk with each other more easily. And a few days on the Colorado will certainly give them solid skills in rafting down rivers together.

But the chances are, no matter how involved the exercise, once the boss and the SMT members return to the office, all of them will revert to the pattern we saw with Dave in Chapter One. The CEO will feel the need to consult with a close group of advisers about major decisions, and the long-term effectiveness of the Senior Management Team as a body will not have changed one iota.

The abiding interest in team building lies in the origins of industrial psychology. In *The Management Myth*, former consultant Matthew Stewart provides a caustic history of this discipline. Its foundation remains the famous Hawthorne experiments conducted in the late 1920s and early 1930s at a Western Electric plant in Illinois and associated with the name Elton Mayo. Researchers isolated six telephone assemblers from their coworkers and made various changes in their working conditions, hoping to identify factors such as lighting, rest breaks, and wage incentives that influenced productivity. Every improvement did appear to increase productivity.

The Hawthorne Experiment became the touchstone for what I call organizational behavioralists (to distinguish them from the *behaviorists*, who are associated with the work of B. F. Skinner and his followers). What put Hawthorne at the center for the behavioralists was the finding that productivity also increased when lighting, rest breaks, and financial incentives were cut back. Although the real cause of these inconclusive results lay in poor experiment design and other distortions introduced by the researchers, Mayo grandly concluded that productivity went up in all circumstances owing to the workers' feelings of involvement. Over the next fifty years the human relations movement, as it came to be called, extended this idea and asserted a direct connection between creating a feeling of belonging and increasing productivity.

Little wonder that consultants, reared on these theories for the past half century, would see team building as the royal road to improved performance—not just for workers but also for executives. "Productivity can be maximized most effectively if the team first increases its overall team intelligence and positivity," says the Web site of a contemporary consultancy that promises to improve management team effectiveness by bringing to bear research from, among other fields, positive psychology and emotional intelligence.

Depending on the leanings of the consultant, various factors are identified that contribute to improved team effectiveness. The following description, from a major human resource consultancy, is typical: "Successful teams become stronger when members learn to work together. They have clear, acceptable goals. The members trust and respect one another. They communicate often and openly. Members have talent for creating and implementing ideas. The leader 'fits' the needs of the team. And the support and resources from the wider organization and community are provided." In other words, team building leads to a more smoothly functioning team.

But does team building increase the impact of the SMT on business performance? Does team building lead to the ability of senior management teams to make better decisions or to make decisions more autonomously? Does team building put the SMT back at the center of the decision-making process? Shaun Gilmore, president of Biomedical Services for the American Red Cross, recalled a typical team-building experience with a previous employer this way: "The boss made good decisions, but he didn't seek input. So, at the CEO's insistence, they brought in a coach, who came to some of our meetings. [The boss] tried to learn to listen better. It was a charade. The boss wasn't going to change what had made him successful, and the idea was to make it a more high-performing team from a teaming perspective, not from a results perspective."

After the Shrinks Have Gone

No matter how much team members trust each other or how much better they communicate, the conflicts in CIO Dave's situation will still arise. All the parties—Dave, the CEO, and the head of the division building the plant in China—honestly believe that they are pursuing a common good. Their disagreement is about who decides what, and when. It's a problem for a political scientist, not a psychologist. The issues that need to be addressed are about power and process, not psyches.

Consider the case of a Brazilian division of a global industrial products company. Executives from the division had devised a strategy to corner a competitor and realize a sustainable share gain in a highly competitive market. The strategy was creative, ambitious, and relatively challenging to execute, but well worth the effort if it succeeded.

The SMT, consisting of the division president and his staff of five, unanimously approved the strategy. Everyone agreed it was a brilliant plan, and team members left the meeting in full accord that the group that had proposed the business case should implement it immediately. Speed was of the essence—this was a top-priority initiative.

Within weeks, the division president was getting calls from the group responsible for deploying the strategy. Resources it had been counting on were tied up on other projects. Plant capacity it needed had been absorbed by other product groups. Regional marketing funds built into the business plan had been redeployed elsewhere.

The president was deeply disappointed in his SMT members. They had let him down. He was spending hours on the phone keeping a project on track that each of them, sitting at the leadership table, had fully committed to weeks before. Among the five of them, every resource of the organization had been represented. All five had agreed to the project. Yet it was the president who was burning up the phone lines to shake loose resources to get the project back on track. He felt something was clearly wrong—something deep and vital—with his team.

It so happened that the SMT was scheduled to have an offsite within weeks of my meeting with the president. He asked if he should bring in someone to work on teamwork. Or accountability. Or keeping to commitments. All his suggestions involved behaviors. All were the province of psychologists and team builders.

If he had turned half his upcoming offsite over to a behavioralist, he might have felt better and the team would probably have learned a few things. But in the long run, would the problem he had just faced have reoccurred? Without question. Because the root cause— what was making his phone ring off the hook—had nothing to do with teamwork, accountability, or commitments. Its roots didn't actually lie with his team at all.

My client was in the midst of a breakdown of management process—the failure to surface and resolve critical resource dependencies when the plan was first considered—but to him it looked like poor leadership behaviors on the part of his team members.

Team building does no harm. After the psychological consultant has gone, the members of the team may get along better; they may be more empathetic or more open. And for personally difficult members of the team, a leadership consultant may be just the thing. But no matter how much comity or collegiality has been achieved, the same old problems begin to resurface.

You could call this process Whac-a-Mole or, to use language of the shrinks themselves, the return of the repressed. As a CEO whose team members had been through plenty of team building put it, "They still fight like kids." The temptation is to see the fighting as a psychological problem and do more team building—or to make team building an ongoing program. But as MasterCard CEO Ajay Banga sees it, it's not a psychological problem but a problem of leadership:

> Often a CEO who is unable to confront the circumstances of the team in a direct way will bring in an outside individual who supposedly has no agenda and who therefore should be able to encourage the eight or ten people to work better together through a series of dynamic team exercises or role plays. You play each

other's shrink, talk about your deepest fears about each other, and so on. But the outsider is brought in because the leader is unwilling to beat the heads together in the room that need to be beaten together. So they opt for a more diplomatic, less confrontational, less direct way of finding a solution. It's a cop-out.

Sometimes, says Sean Moriarty, former CEO of Ticketmaster, the problem is simply the state of the business itself: "If you're bringing psychologists in because the team and culture you have is not the team and culture you want, you're doomed to failure. I would argue that most external resources deployed to help solve for team-related issues are in reality being deployed against dysfunctional businesses, and they can't be fixed."

Nevertheless, leaders continue to call in the psychologists to work on team building—and they continue to be disappointed with the results. The behavioralists have a ready response: the team is only half of the problem. The other half is the leader. If the top of the organization isn't functioning effectively, perhaps the boss should take a good, hard look in the mirror and change the way he or she leads.

CHAPTER 3

Don't Blame the Boss

The amount of effort devoted to changing the behavior of leaders dwarfs that aimed at team building. It includes a vast army of consultants, an ocean of academic literature, and an unending stream of popular books and articles about the ways leaders can improve themselves. A search on the term *leadership* on Amazon.com produced over 67,000 titles—more than twice as many as for the word *profit*.

It has always struck me as odd that as executives achieve higher levels of success in an organization, the pressure only increases on them to change aspects of their leadership style—often those very aspects that got them to their current roles in the first place.

The behavioralists find the leverage irresistible—given the importance and power of the leader relative to the members of the team, it stands to reason that the leader's behavior could be a prime reason why a senior team is performing less than optimally. If other measures have, in the long term, not resulted in a significantly better team, straightening out the boss should go a long way toward straightening out the entire team. All it takes, behavioralists would tell us, is a change in the leader's style.

In Search of the Ideal Leader

In 1939, psychologist Kurt Lewin, one of the fathers of today's fields of organizational behavior and change management, did some pioneering research into the psychology of leadership. From his study of adolescent boys, Lewin concluded that there are three basic leadership styles: *authoritarian*, *democratic*, and *laissez-faire* (or *delegative*). The authoritarian leader centralizes power in himself and makes all important decisions. The democratic leader solicits the advice and counsel of subordinates, encourages participation by stakeholders, and at least attempts consensus before making a decision. The laissez-faire, or delegative, leader avoids making decisions on his own, ceding a great deal of autonomy to subordinates and letting them implement decisions in whatever way they think best.

Lewin's powerful notion of leadership styles lives on in many subsequent approaches to leadership. There is, for example, the *transformational* leader—the charismatic politician or celebrity CEO—who infuses the team with his or her values and inspires followers to adopt the leader's vision. At the other end of the spectrum are approaches like Douglas McGregor's Theory Y, which position the leader's job as helping other people fulfill their potential—an idea carried forward into today's *servant leadership*. Leadership consultants devote much time and effort to uncovering various styles of leadership behavior, defining an optimal style managers should aim for, and then trying to help those managers get to that desired model.

The concept of leadership traits also continues to play a major role in executive recruiting and succession planning. Corporations spend a fortune on consultants who assess and address the strengths and weaknesses of individual managers through one-on-one interventions and a battery of standardized tests. Although some of this work aims at helping individuals deal with personal issues, like maintaining work-life balance or becoming a better listener, most is directed outward—toward making executives better leaders. And so the corridors of power are clogged with consultants, coaches, and psychologists, all attempting to build a stronger cadre of leaders at the top of the organization.

Though these behavioralist theorists, popularizers, and practitioners would insist that their differences are at least as great as their similarities, four broad assumptions drive their work:

- *There is a range of leadership styles.* Terminologies differ, depending on the theorist or practitioner, but when it comes to profiling leadership characteristics, most of the behavioralists offer a spectrum of styles that can be traced back to Lewin's original formulation.

- *Leaders must find the style that best suits them.* The idea of a range of styles carries over to the titles of leadership books available for those seeking role models. Amazon.com lists numerous titles that begin with the phrase *"Leadership Secrets of ..."* followed by a name—everyone from Attila the Hun (who, I suppose, was on the autocratic end of the spectrum) to Jesus (I haven't read the book, but I would bet he isn't depicted as autocratic). From *Leadership Secrets of Hillary Clinton* to *Leadership Secrets from Jack Welch* to *Leadership Secrets of Genghis Khan* (for those who might find Attila the Hun not quite right for them), the assumption is that there's a public or historical figure whose style, if correctly mirrored, can help you pave the path to success.

- *The key to success as a leader is to find a style and stick to it.* The leader molds his or her behavior to a consciously selected set of standards and "walks the talk" of a certain type of leadership so that subordinates will see a new and improved individual, and the team and organization will improve as a result.

- *The democratic or inclusive style is the most desirable.* Lewin was writing when Hitler, Mussolini, and Tojo held sway in the Axis powers. His choice of names for his decision styles was no accident. The enormous cultural baggage carried by the terms *authoritarian* and *democratic* in Lewin's day has been brought forward into our own era of political correctness. It's no wonder leaders see themselves as needing to be democratic; there is an inherent bias that involving teams in decisions is somehow morally superior to running organizations along authoritarian lines.

In the 1970s, tacking against the powerful tide of these assumptions came a new perspective offered by a former teacher of mine—Victor Vroom, the John G. Searle Professor of Organization and Management at Yale. Vic saw that Lewin's model was driving a bias toward democratic decision making, resulting in sweeping behavioralist claims such as "the authoritarian style should normally only be used on rare occasions."

He argued that decisions are required in many very different situations and that the context itself largely drives the type of decision-making behavior required. The idea seems almost self-evident today, but it flew in the face of the behavioralists who competed to put forward their individual (and often conflicting) models of what they saw as the optimal leadership style.

Inside the Box

I'll never forget the first lecture of Vic's I attended. He was demonstrating a device he called the Vroom box. It was a small, handheld wooden box, with a set of push buttons and light bulbs on the top. By pushing the buttons in particular sequences and correctly interpreting the various combinations of lit and unlit bulbs that then occurred, each of us could become a better manager.

Unlike orgone boxes or Dr. Seuss's magical "vroom," the Vroom box had real substance behind it. Vic Vroom was one of the pioneers in the field of organizational behavior, and one of his seminal contributions was the Vroom-Yetton-Jago normative decision model—the model that powered the logic of the Vroom box.

The Vroom-Yetton-Jago normative decision model extended Lewin's model by saying that leaders and their teams can make any particular decision in one of five ways, ranging across a spectrum from highly authoritarian at one extreme to complete delegation at the other:

1. *Autocratic I—decide.* The leader solves the problem alone, using information already available to him.

2. *Autocratic II—consult individuals.* The leader obtains additional information from selected team members and then makes the decision. The team doesn't meet, and some team members may not be informed as the decision is being made.

3. *Consultative I—consult all group members.* The leader shares the problem with each team member individually, asks for information and evaluation, and the leader then decides. The team never discusses the issue.

4. *Consultative II—facilitate.* The team meets, and discusses the problem collectively. The decision, however, is made by the leader. If the group reaches consensus, fine. If not, the leader will make the call. Either way, the leader decides, because consensus cannot be reached unless the leader is in agreement as well.

5. *Group II—delegate.* The leader meets with the group to discuss the situation. The leader focuses and directs the discussion, but does not impose her will. The group, not the leader, makes the final decision.

This model suggests that each of us has a natural preference for making decisions somewhere along this five-point spectrum. Some managers always tend to anchor on one point—extreme examples are, on the one hand, those who seem to delegate every decision to their teams and, on the other hand, those who make every decision themselves without seeking input from anyone about anything. Most of us are comfortable across a spread of two, three, or perhaps four of these decision styles. It's the rare manager who is equally comfortable across the entire spectrum.

Vroom's real breakthrough came in his insistence that different types of decisions call for different decision styles. For example, when Mayor Rudy Giuliani arrived at Ground Zero on the day of the 9/11 tragedy, a consultative decision-making style would not have served him well. In those first few critical hours, the speed and efficiency of an autocratic style was required. By contrast, the boss who chooses to revamp an important human resource policy without seeking the guidance and buy-in of his team could easily gain a reputation as a dictator and end up making bad decisions that run aground on implementation.

How, as a leader, can you match the appropriate style with a particular decision? That's where the Vroom box came in. Vroom had developed a hierarchical series of eight yes-or-no questions that could be answered in order to characterize any individual decision situation. For example:

- Is the technical quality of the decision important?
- Is subordinate commitment to the decision important?
- If you were to make the decision by yourself, is it reasonably certain that your subordinates would be committed to the decision?

By responding to the questions and pushing the appropriate buttons on the Vroom box (or following a structured decision tree), you could, presumably, identify the optimal decision style for any particular decision. The model assumed that sometimes the autocratic style was preferable to the delegative, and sometimes vice versa—and answering the eight questions, in the right sequence, would point to the right decision-making approach for any decision.

Along with the model and the Vroom box, Vroom developed a diagnostic instrument that posed a series of decision scenarios, which he administered to his students as well as to thousands of managers across a wide range of industries and geographies. By indicating how you would respond to a particular situation and modeling those responses against an idealized correct answer, you could gain insight into your personal decision style and be able to answer questions like these: What is my natural decision-style bias? How flexible am I in matching different styles to different decisions? Am I uncomfortable as an autocrat? Is my natural bias toward delegating decisions to a group?

It's a useful model and it leads to an illuminating experience. Different decisions require different approaches. Good managers vary the way they make decisions based on the nature of the decision to be made. Flexibility in decision making is better than inflexibility. What's the best leadership style? The answer: it depends—on the circumstances of the decision and what comes naturally to each manager. Vroom's major contribution to the debate Lewin began was to show that becoming a more effective leader does not necessarily imply changing your style or the way you prefer to make decisions, but it does imply developing enough flexibility to successfully adapt to the demands of the particular type of decision to be made.

The concept of formalizing optimal decision styles by situation and of emphasizing the ability of leaders to flex their styles to adapt swept through the world of leadership consulting. Three decades after I attended the Vroom box lecture, echoes of Vic Vroom's approach still resonate. Leaders are coached to be flexible. They are asked to consider how they adapt to different situations. They are encouraged to take appropriate accountability, involving their team as the situation dictates.

What Vroom shares with the behavioralists is the belief that there is a range of styles, but where he parts company with many of them is over his belief that the effective leader should find and adapt to any style that is optimal for the situation. And he clearly does not think that the delegative style is naturally superior. In fact the diagnostic tool he used to test us described thirty hypothetical situations requiring some type of decision. In his ideal answer set the number of times that the decision belongs entirely to the group is once. And only four of the decision situations call for the leader to step back and neutrally facilitate. Most of the time, the decision is seen to be up to the leader, with or without input from some or all of the leader's team members.

But Vroom's position does remain behavioralist. Improvement focuses on changing behavior—in this case the leader's behavior. Whether great leaders are made or born, getting organizations to raise their performance levels requires the people who lead them to improve. If leaders can just broaden their natural decision-making tendencies, expand their repertoire of behaviors, and get comfortable doing things that they may currently find uncomfortable, things will get better.

As I've noted, leadership coaching and individual performance management have their place. But as with team building, when the shrinks depart the same conflicts and vague dissatisfactions remain. Even in the best cases, where the leader and the team see few problems, the question arises as to why so much of the time of the most valuable executives is wasted in meetings where little of substance is decided.

Do the "Rights" Thing

The failure of the behavioralists to fix the issues of top-team performance implies that the underlying problem with decision making may not be psychological or behavioral at all. But if it isn't a question of the behavior of the team or the behavior of the leader, what is it? Breaking sharply with the behavioralists, a significant number of experts would say that what you need to fix is not the team or the leader but the *process*. The Heidrick & Struggles study notes that "team processes—how a team works together, including its decision-making patterns, modes of conflict management, responsiveness to changes in customer or other environmental changes, and the management of its meetings—are viewed as *the* most important contributor to Top Management Team effectiveness."[1]

The authors of the Heidrick study agree that different decisions require different methods of attack, but instead of addressing decisions from the point of view of the leader's repertoire of behaviors, they argue that it is more effective to establish a set of clear processes—starting with decision making. Clarify who gets involved, when, and what their decision rights are at any given point in the formulation of the decision. Then chart that involvement for each kind of decision. Once the process is made clear, the team's ability to function effectively within that process will presumably be enhanced.

Decision rights emerged from the responsibility charting frequently used as a tool in project management. For example, one of the most commonly used such tools, RACI charting, identifies the team **R**esponsible for doing a particular piece of work, the individual **A**ccountable for seeing that the work is done, the individuals or groups who should be **C**onsulted for their opinions about the work, and the individuals or groups who should be **I**nformed as the work takes place.

Similar frameworks, appropriately adapted for the particular requirements of decision making, may be used to chart decision rights. Consultants Paul Rogers and Marcia Blenko, of Bain & Company, for example, suggest the RAPID approach,[2] in which each person involved in the decision-making process is assigned one of five decision-making roles:

- **Recommend.** Recommenders gather and assess the relevant facts, obtaining input from appropriate parties, and then recommend a decision or action.

- **Agree.** Agreers formally approve a recommendation and can delay it if more work is required.
- **Perform.** Performers are accountable for making a decision happen once it's been made.
- **Input.** Inputers combine facts and judgment to provide input into a recommendation.
- **Decide.** Deciders make the ultimate decision and commit the organization to action.

Unquestionably, making decision rights clear and putting those rights where they belong can improve performance. I use it often with my clients in order to clarify the roles both of individuals and of groups in key processes. For example, when reviewing the agenda for a planned strategy offsite with the meeting owner, I often ask what the specific purpose is in having the team review each section of the material: "Are you informing them of something that is already locked and loaded? Are you looking for input so that you can make changes if necessary? Are you trying to have the team surface likely issues that you will face in implementation? Are you having them develop their individual roles so that implementation will succeed?" The most common response to these questions is, "I'm not sure." *Why am I here?* isn't just a question freshmen ask in a philosophy class. Often the same question is running through the minds of Senior Management Team (SMT) members when the room is dark and the PowerPoint display is up on the screen.

Understanding where in the decision-making process various stakeholders ought to weigh in is critical to the smooth operation of an enterprise, especially in today's matrixed organizations. Clear roles in a well-defined decision-making process can encourage a coordinated, productive debate that incorporates valuable input from multiple sources, which can lead to higher-quality decisions. Thus the proponents of decision rights, like the behavioralists and the proponents of adaptable leadership styles, have a real contribution to make.

However, in all three cases, the contribution comes with a significant limitation:

- The behavioralists are right in sensing that there is a problem with the top team, but wrong in seeing it as psychological.

- The proponents of varying one's leadership style are right in pointing out that different kinds of decisions require different approaches to decision making, but wrong in seeing this as an issue of the leader's behavior.

- The proponents of decision rights are correct in seeing that role clarity is important in decision making, but wrong in thinking that the remedy lies merely in clarifying the SMT's decision rights.

More important, beyond these contributions and drawbacks, all three camps—and virtually all researchers into Senior Management Teams—share a crucial unexamined assumption that constitutes an even greater weakness in their attempts to address the perceived problems of the senior team. That assumption is one of the central myths about organizations that nobody ever seems to question, especially not the myriad experts trying to fix senior teams and leaders. And it is the major myth that this book was written to dispel. Simply stated, it is the widespread belief that Senior Management Teams are, or should be, decision-making bodies.

To be fair, the decision rights advocates do indicate a single Decider, as in the RAPID approach, or Accountable person, as in the RACI method. But they also clearly advocate the heavy involvement of teams in decision making. For example, Rogers and Blenko remark in discussing the RAPID approach that the "person with the D is the formal decision maker. He or she is ultimately accountable for the decision, for better or worse, and has the authority to resolve any impasse in the decision-making process and to commit the organization to action."[3]

So, even though formal decision authority is seen to rest with one person, the implication of all these models is that teams should make decisions, with the leader stepping in "for better or worse" to "resolve any impasse." But as we will see in the next chapter, the nature of the SMT makes this assumption untenable at the top of organizations. Senior Management Teams—again for reasons that go largely unexamined—are in fact not well suited for making most major decisions.

Notes

1. Rich Rosen and Fred Adair, *How CEOs and Top Management Team Members* Really *See Their Performance* (Chicago: Heidrick & Struggles International Inc., 2008), p. 5. Internal document. Used by permission.
2. Paul Rogers and Marcia Blenko, "Who has the D? How Clear Decision Roles Enhance Organizational Performance," *Harvard Business Review* (January 2006), pp. 52–61.
3. Rogers and Blenko, "Who has the D?" p. 58.

CHAPTER 4

Four Fundamental Conflicts at the Heart of Senior Management Teams

As we've seen in the previous two chapters, the sources of the dissatisfaction or vague disappointment with the effectiveness of the senior management team (SMT) on the part of leaders and team members don't lie in the psyche. The problem isn't faulty interpersonal dynamics within the team. It's also not the leadership style of the CEO. In fact the problem is rooted in a fundamental tension between the assumption that the SMT is, or should be, a decision-making body and the fact that the very nature of the SMT makes it largely ill suited to that task. As we saw in Chapter One, this tension often surfaces when the CEO and the SMT are dealing with a business case that the CEO has already decided to approve. The CEO's call for a final review by the SMT implies that the team makes decisions as a team, but the review then consists of a ritualistic nodding through of the case, which is a tacit admission that the team doesn't make such decisions. By their nature, SMTs entail four fundamental conflicts—not one of which is psychological—that make the team's status as a decision-making body highly problematical:

- **Mission Control versus Knights of the Round Table**. In team discussions, members are torn between the functional expertise that brought them to their place at the table and the leader's desire that they take an organization-wide, holistic perspective. This is a conflict between what the leader expects of them and what they know.

- **The team versus the legislature**. It's called a *team*, but it more closely resembles a *legislature*. Each team member represents a significant constituency—all the people in the member's function or business area—constituents who aren't present at SMT meetings. Meanwhile the CEO expects team members to act in the best interests of the overall enterprise. This is a conflict of accountability.

- **The House versus the Senate**. What kind of legislature the team resembles is undefined, resulting in deliberations clouded with ambiguity. Is it a group like the U.S. Senate, where every state has equal weight, or is it more like the U.S. House of Representatives, in which the most populous states have the most clout? This is a conflict about where the balance of power is within the team.

- **The majority versus the majority**. The *voting paradox*, first demonstrated by a French mathematician and social theorist, the Marquis de Condorcet, in the eighteenth century, shows that no matter what choice a group makes, other alternatives can simultaneously command a majority of the group's preferences. This is a conflict about consensus.

None of the first three of these conflicts is easily resolved—and the voting paradox cannot be resolved at all. But all of them can be easily understood. That understanding can help both leaders and team members let go of unrealistic expectations about the executive team's role. The leader can better manage the tensions to which these inevitable conflicts give rise. The team can focus not on smooth functioning—that's the true realm of team building—but on finding the things it can do best.

Mission Control Versus Knights of the Round Table: Functional Specialists or Reflections of the CEO?

Those of us of a certain age remember the Mission Control Center. During the first decade of the space program, every time a NASA spacecraft was set to blast off, a boxy, black-and-white television was wheeled into our schoolrooms so that we could watch the scene live.

We'd see the rocket on the pad at Cape Canaveral being fueled prior to launch. The TV cameras would take us into Mission Control in Houston, a room full of men (yes, they were all men) wearing headsets, each glued to a console with a label on top—CAPCOM or SURGEON or GUIDANCE—which we learned to translate as such functions as telemetry or medical or meteorology. At the center of the room, providing the control in Mission Control, was Gene Kranz, NASA's flight director—crew cut, white shirt, skinny tie, military bearing—the man with total authority to make the life-and-death decision to unleash a spacecraft from its pad.

As the countdown progressed, a constant stream of information came in from each of the men at those consoles. Weather holds would be placed on the countdown. Computers would need to be reset. Radio systems and medical data were being constantly evaluated. Just before the final countdown, Kranz would turn to the leader of each of the major systems for a final check. "Telemetry?" Go. "Meteorology?" Go. "Medical?" Go. Once he had a sign-off from each of his primary crew heads, the final countdown would commence—"10, 9, 8, ..." until we all watched in wonder as the massive rocket lifted off.

Mission Control provides a model of the functionally oriented SMT in its purest form. Each member of the team focuses on the issues that pertain to his or her area of specialization and the leader, before setting the launch into motion, checks one last time with key lieutenants—*speak now or forever hold your peace.*

It is not the model that most CEOs favor. Dave, the chief information officer (CIO) we met in Chapter One, and his colleague Susan, the human resource head, aren't alone in being asked to put on their corporate hats and take a holistic perspective in SMT meetings. Members of SMTs have told me repeatedly that in meetings where critical business decisions are being discussed, they are almost always enjoined to take the CEO's perspective.

Says the head of HR for a Fortune 500 company, "My CEO would hate it if I started with, 'well, from an HR perspective,' every time I spoke up. If you can't take the generalist perspective, you get a demerit. He expects all of us to be business generalists." Like Susan, many have learned that it's wiser not to raise functional issues when the CEO wants someone looking at issues from the "holistic," "company-wide," or "silo-free" perspective.

I have asked numerous CEOs where on a scale of 1 to 10 they wanted the members of their teams to fall, with a 1 being pure functionalists and a 10 being people with a holistic perspective. This reply from the former CEO of a Fortune 500 multinational is typical: "I don't want anybody to come and sit at that table who can't play the generalist role. I want somebody who has demonstrated leadership, demonstrated results, who's multifunctional, multinational, and has presence. I know I'll never get all 10s at the table, but God help someone who's only a specialist. I want people who are thinking about the company, who recognize that they are the leaders for the company first and secondly bring expertise in a particular area or watch that they're responsible for."

Says the CEO of another Fortune 500 company: "I know they have functional jobs, but I generally don't want a detailed functional answer. I want a strategic answer. At this level we're talking about creating a strategic advantage—not doing project management."

None of the CEOs I interviewed said they expect SMT members to be mini-CEOs 100 percent of the time, of course. There are times in these meetings when team members inevitably speak with their functional hats on. But the amount of airtime that the functional perspective gets is minimal, as my firm found in research we recently completed involving CEOs, their leadership teams, and the functioning of those teams. Among the questions we asked senior executives was this one: "What percentage of the time would you estimate you are typically expected to take the overall corporate perspective versus the functional perspective in Senior Management Team meetings?" Their responses revealed that 75 to 90 percent of the time they were expected to take the generalist perspective of the CEO. They were expected to take a functional view only 10 to 25 percent of the time.

Those findings confirm my experience. In three decades of work with leadership teams, I've never heard a single boss say of team members, "I wish they would spend more time in these meetings wearing their functional hats." Or even, "I'm sure glad there's one place where all the different parts of the organization come together so I can hear from multiple organizational perspectives."

From a CEO's point of view, executives are not on the SMT to provide functional expertise but, most of the time, to act as the nine or ten wise people of the corporation, providing top-level guidance and advice to the CEO. Says Sean Moriarty, former CEO of Ticketmaster, "It comes down to being able to contribute to a dialogue beyond just your functional area of oversight."

Clearly, what many CEOs want, far from the Mission Control model, is something more akin to King Arthur's Knights of the Round Table. According to legend the table was round to signify that each knight was of equal value, differing little from the other knights or even from the king himself. And why not? Sir Lancelot, Sir Galahad, and the rest had proved themselves many times and often shown as much mettle in strategy and battle as Arthur himself.

But the members of a typical SMT aren't all knights. Most of them aren't even general managers, like the CEO. They mostly represent support functions. Over time they have earned the right, through some highly developed and specialist skills, to lead a division, a functional area, or some other major domain in the company. Trying to make them all generalists who can take a CEO's perspective doesn't play to their strengths. In being asked to take the CEO's view they are being forced to suppress what they know and do best. Yet for most of the time in SMT meetings that is just what is happening; they are being asked to assume the role of knights. It's not surprising that the result should be frustration—frustration on the part of both team members and leaders—or that many leadership team meetings are Kabuki-like pageants of ritual agreement.

In my experience, CEOs, who mean well and have the best of intentions, are often shocked to find out how some people react to a boss's desire for a holistic perspective from individual team members. Some years ago I was cofacilitating a strategy offsite with one of the best consultants I've ever known—I'll call her Sarah. The CEO of the company, with no prior warning to Sarah or me, kicked off the offsite by saying, "During the next couple of days I want everyone to try to see the company broadly—do your best to look at these issues through my eyes, not through the filter of your division or function."

During the first break Sarah pulled the CEO aside and minced no words. "Imagine," she said, "if we told them that during the upcoming session everyone is going to look through the eyes of Sales. Then at future sessions we're all going to take the perspective of Finance and then of Operations and so on. I think it's fair to say that it doesn't make sense. And it's egocentric to ask them to look at the world through your eyes. They can only look through their eyes. We should be listening for their perspectives, not trying to get them to mimic yours. That's the strength of this team."

The CEO, a thoughtful and successful leader, looked genuinely surprised. "I thought that taking a holistic perspective would bring out the best in them. It never occurred to me that it might be regarded as egocentric. I thought it would be regarded as inclusive and collegial." When the meeting resumed he graciously reversed himself. Smiling and nodding in Sarah's direction, he said that "on the advice of counsel" he wanted to refocus the meeting on getting the benefit of each participant's unique perspective on the issues to be discussed.

In expecting all SMT members to be knights, CEOs diminish the collective capability of their teams to do what they do best, which is to bring to the table the great benefit of their technical expertise in the areas they represent. Undeniably, there will be talented executives on the team who have the ability to take the CEO's perspective. These gifted leaders may be candidates to become CEO themselves someday. In fact many CEOs I talked to said that they see participation in the SMT as partly a developmental activity for team members. But there is no reason to suppose that the entire SMT is made up of future CEOs—or that mastering the CEO perspective is a desirable developmental goal for every one of them—and thereby squander the real collective strength of the team.

When they are asked to take off their functional hats, executives are thrown into a chaotic gray zone where they are denied their platform of functional expertise yet are expected to comment on (and criticize) activities about which they have no special knowledge and which lie in the domain of a colleague. The result is often confusion, unproductive conversations, and frustration all around. And as any seasoned executive knows, no sensible person lobs grenades into another team member's territory. "The only reason a CEO wants people mucking around in each other's business," says one such executive, "is that he doesn't want to do it himself."

That doesn't mean SMT members should entirely abandon their attempt to see the big picture. There are often times when it's perfectly appropriate for them to take a holistic view. But to make the most of the SMT's abilities, the amount of time spent on the holistic perspective versus the functional perspective should be reversed. Instead of devoting 75 to 90 percent of their time in SMT meetings to the CEO's perspective, the team members could far more productively devote that percentage of time to providing the perspectives of their functions or divisions—and in that way produce more value from their collective efforts.

The Team Versus the Legislature: The Representative from Finance, the Senator from Operations

The conflict between the roles of functional expert and generalist is complicated by another feature of SMTs, one that is not just a matter of expertise or of the leader's expectations. Looked at through the eyes of a political scientist, the SMT more closely resembles a legislature than it does a team. We may refer to it as an *executive team* because it is a group made up of executives, but its members could also be thought of as the Senator from Operations, the Distinguished Member from Marketing, the Representative from Finance, and so on. Each represents a powerful constituency in the organization, and most or all of them are at the table because of the role they currently fill, not because of any innate quality they have as individuals. If the head of Marketing or the head of a division disappeared tomorrow, a new individual would be in the vacated SMT seat the next day, representing that same constituency.

With each member serving as a voice for a different function or division, each vying for resources and influence, it's not surprising that the SMT's activities more closely resemble legislative deliberations than teamwork. As CIO Dave found, SMT members are expected by the people, divisions, and departments they represent to speak up for their interests.

Consider the likely scenario when Dave holds his next IT leadership meeting. He informs his staff of the decision about the plant expansion in China, and he says, "I don't need to tell you that our plans for the year just changed."

No, he doesn't. They know very well that the strategies, the budget, and personnel plans that they spent four months working through have been blown to smithereens. They're likely to be stretched to the breaking point by the combination of their responsibilities for the China plant and an upgrade of the company's enterprise resource planning (ERP) system scheduled to take place at the same time. They won't be able to do an adequate job of either. And when glitches appear in the ERP implementation, they'll be held accountable. They voice their concerns, some with an edge in their tone that suggests their CIO has let them down—that in some way their interests must have been inadequately represented during the approval process.

Dave doesn't blame them for being unhappy. In fact he feels torn between what the CEO wants and what the IT team expects. The CEO wants him to consider the good of the whole whereas the IT team members expect him to represent their concerns and point of view. He's in much the same position as a member of Congress who's torn between what might be good for the country overall and what might be good for the folks back in her district.

Yet most of the time in SMT meetings, these business area representatives are expected to shed their "parochial" concerns. And in the case of the CIO and the China plant expansion, he had no chance to take the business case back to his constituents and validate it with them.

There is an added complication. Although SMT members represent their various constituencies, they don't vote on important decisions. Says Steve Maritz, chairman and CEO of Maritz Holdings Inc., "Everyone has a chance to weigh in, and there are lots of times when everyone's opinions are sought, but I can't ever remember a vote taking place."

Neither can I. In all of my years of experience, I've yet to encounter an SMT in the for-profit world that took a genuine vote. Participants may do some informal polling or go around the table expressing their views—often in response to a CEO's vague, "Well, what do you think?" But a binding vote where the majority rules? Never. As a result, they don't even have a real legislator's ready defense when the constituents are unhappy about a decision: "As the record shows, I voted no."

The House Versus the Senate: Are Some More Equal Than Others?

Although members of an SMT rarely vote, they undoubtedly have vastly differing political weights within their organization. The head of a large division, a chief operating officer, or a Sales Department head may have large numbers of employees with enormous impact on revenue or profitability. The chief financial officer may have control over budgets and investments. But what about the heads of smaller businesses or of HR or Legal? They may have great authority over a limited domain and great personal influence, but their overall power on the team is often outweighed by that of their colleagues.

Because executives on the SMT are considered peers, it's easy to assume that a functional head on the team carries as much weight in meetings as an operational executive and that small operations can expect the same voice at the table as large ones. But when it comes time to discuss important issues, ambiguity often reigns. Is the team like the U.S. Senate, where every state is equally represented? Or is it like the House of Representatives, where the influence of Florida, Texas, or California overtly outweighs that of far less populous states, like Rhode Island, North Dakota, or Delaware? Although the rules and decision processes of the Senate and House are clear, with political weights balanced in one chamber and deliberately unbalanced in the other, the situation within an SMT is far murkier.

Bob Selander, retired president and CEO of MasterCard, seems to affirm that it is a team of equals. "I think that at the end of the day it's more of a Senate," he says. But he quickly adds, "If you have somebody on the team who is responsible for $2 billion in revenue and he says that this course of action is really going to affect his unit adversely or positively, then you're more likely to take that into consideration than if it came from someone with $100 million in revenue."

This ambivalence, expressed by a number of CEOs I talked to, reflects on the one hand an understandable wish for collegiality and equality on the team and on the other hand a recognition of reality. Ellyn McColgan, former president and chief operating officer of Morgan Stanley Global Wealth Management Group, recalls an experience she had at a previous employer. "I was managing an organization of thousands of people in a high-growth environment and we were drowning in issues. The head of Legal would come into staff meetings and talk on and on about his thirty-five people and the progress they were making with team building. I went to my CEO and said, 'I have thousands of employees. You cannot expect me to act as if I am interested in the interpersonal dynamics of his thirty-five-person department.' The truth is that all levels of responsibility are not created equal."

Because it's often unclear whether the Senate or the House model is in play, it can be difficult to understand what is really taking place. Are the more powerful members brokering a decision? Was a decision brokered before the meeting started? Often this lack of clarity not only gets in the way of using the SMT appropriately but also creates destructive dynamics in discussions. The more powerful members—the New York and California representatives—remain silent during the meeting, secure in the knowledge that they can buttonhole the CEO afterward and privately argue their position. Subsequently, when the course of action bears little resemblance to what was discussed in the meeting, other members of the team wonder retrospectively about its purpose. Was it a charade? Was it recreational? Did the CEO simply change her mind? Or as so often happens, did she have her mind changed by one of their more powerful colleagues?

The Majority Versus the Majority: The Impossibility of Deciding

Although most SMTs don't formally vote on big decisions, that doesn't mean that their members don't have preferences in regard to issues under discussion. Some preferences among the members for one option or another exist implicitly. Even in those Kabuki-like meetings when a decision is being nodded through, team members have opinions, whether they express them or not. Though the individual preferences remain uncounted, this unspoken allocation of votes is as real as if the members had been polled. For example, two members who have initiated a particular course of action strongly favor it; three other members favor a diametrically opposed course of action, though they don't say so; the rest of the team prefers to do nothing. And in those instances when informal polling of the members takes place, the preferences become explicit.

But whether preferences are expressed or unexpressed, the real problem is that reaching collective decisions based on individual preferences is very nearly impossible. As mentioned previously, this phenomenon was first noted by the Marquis de Condorcet in the eighteenth century. His voting paradox demonstrated that when a group of three or more people sets priorities among three or more items, majority wishes can be in conflict with each other. Despite operating in a completely rational way, a group of three or more can hold two or more majority viewpoints at the same time.

Most people remember the transitive law from mathematics: if $A > B$ and $B > C$, then $A > C$. It's a principle of logic as well. If I prefer vanilla ice cream over chocolate and chocolate over strawberry, then, if I'm behaving rationally—that is, according to the transitive law—I prefer vanilla over strawberry. In fact the transitive law holds not only for individuals but for pairs of people as well. But Condorcet's paradox demonstrates that the transitive law breaks down for groups of three or more. It's perfectly possible, in a group setting, for A > B, B > C, and C > A to all be true.

A simple example illustrates the implications for management of Condorcet's voting paradox. I like to call this example "The Boss Is Always Wrong." A three-member management team is attempting to select a fleet vehicle for the company. Given the choice of BMW, Lexus, and Mercedes, the individual team members vote as shown in Table 4.1.

To break the impasse, the boss might intervene and choose BMW, but as the table shows, two-thirds of the team would prefer Lexus. The boss might choose Lexus, but two-thirds of the team would prefer Mercedes. And finally the boss might choose Mercedes, but two-thirds of the team would prefer BMW. Instead of being transitive—BMW beats Lexus, Lexus beats Mercedes, and therefore BMW beats Mercedes—the choice is cyclic. Mercedes beats BMW.

You would naturally expect that given three choices a majority of this team might not agree on a top choice. But Condorcet's paradox goes much further. It's possible that not only will there be no good answer but also that whatever choice the boss makes will be opposed by two-thirds of the team preferring one of the other options.

This phenomenon arises because majorities for each possible alternative can arise from different subsets of the group, and then they will conflict. Almost 300 years after Condorcet, economist

Table 4.1: Illustration of the Voting Paradox

Person	First choice	Second choice	Third choice
Lou	BMW	Mercedes	Lexus
Sue	Mercedes	Lexus	BMW
Stu	Lexus	BMW	Mercedes

Kenneth Arrow was awarded the Nobel Prize in economics, in part for his *impossibility theorem*, which established that no preference voting system can be designed to circumvent the voting paradox. It's impossible, Arrow showed, for groups to be rational in terms of preferences in the same way that individuals and pairs are.

Consider a nine-person leadership team that wants to cut costs and is weighing three options:

A. Close plants.

B. Move from a direct sales force to distributors.

C. Reduce benefits and pay.

Although any individual executive may be able to "rack and stack" his or her individual preferences, it's possible for a majority to be found for each alternative simultaneously. Five members might prefer closing plants to moving sales to distributors (A > B). A different set of five might prefer moving sales to reducing benefits and pay (B > C). By the transitive property, closing plants should be preferred to reducing benefits and pay (A > C). But the paradox is that five members could rank reducing benefits and pay over closing plants (C > A). Instead of being transitive, the preferences will then be circular. No matter which option is chosen, only a minority of team members will agree with it, and it's likely that different majorities will prefer alternative outcomes. Moreover, as Arrow demonstrated, no voting method—not allocation of points to alternatives, not rank ordering of choices, nothing—can solve the problem.

Each individual in adopting preferences can be behaving perfectly rationally and in full accord with the transitive law. In choosing A over B and B over C, I am also choosing A over C. But because that law doesn't apply to a group of three or more, the logic can become circular. As a result, the behavior of the group *as a group* appears to be irrational. Before long the psychologists are called in to fix a problem that could only be cured by repealing a law of mathematics.

Although Condorcet's paradox and Arrow's impossibility theorem are well understood in political science and economics, these concepts haven't yet crossed over to practical management. Understanding the voting paradox can greatly alter the way an SMT regards its function, especially to the extent that its members see it as a decision-making body. Even in the overwhelming majority of cases, in which votes are not taken, this understanding could help explain and dispel what is likely to be some degree of unhappiness among some team members about any decision. And it certainly helps explain the situation felt at times by many bosses—that whatever choice they make seems to be perceived as the wrong one.

Maybe the Problem Is That There Is No Problem

Any of these four phenomena—the specialist versus generalist tension, the group's legislative underpinnings, the unclear distribution of power, or the sheer impossibility of groups deciding— can result in what appear to be behavioral problems or team dysfunction but in reality all four reflect the inherent structural tensions of all SMTs. Functional heads, leery of appearing parochial, may suppress function-based concerns in discussions and perfunctorily go along with whatever is on the table. The responsibility of representing one's function or unit while also looking out for the overall best interests of the enterprise might result in the kind of horse-trading outside the room that blurs and blunts initiatives. The Rhode Islands and Delawares of the team, assuming an equality that doesn't exist, might take up inordinate airtime or resent the power of the New Yorks and Californias.

But whatever psychological reactions, if any, these tensions might provoke—resentment, resignation, or even indifference— the solution is not psychological; the answer is not team building; the problem is not the boss. Behavioralist attempts to increase the effectiveness of teams can't resolve these four causes of SMT ineffectiveness. Although SMTs are excellent forums for brainstorming, creativity, option development, information sharing, coordination, dependency management, and a host of other functions, they are often ill suited to decision making, even of the casual, consensus-seeking type that characterizes the deliberations of many senior teams.

It's time to stop blaming the SMT or the leader for the failure of the team to effectively raise and resolve critical issues. Time to abandon the myth that we find in most organizations and in almost any book, popular or academic, on the subject of SMTs: the assumption that there is one monolithic team at the top that should be responsible for making most of an organization's critical decisions.

Why not instead accept the reality that the use of kitchen cabinets points toward: CEOs need different configurations of people—different people in the room—for different types of decisions and different tasks. Why not forthrightly acknowledge that fact and explicitly use a portfolio of teams to help you run the company or your organizational area? That doesn't mean disbanding the leadership team. It means abandoning unrealizable tasks for the team, such as making major decisions, and opening the way to even higher and better uses, the most important of which are described in Part Two of this book.

Instead of assuming that a single management team of direct reports can best handle most issues, great leaders surround themselves with a portfolio of teams—permanent and ad hoc—to draw upon. Rather than seeing themselves as the organization chart depicts them—leading from the top of a pyramid, with the SMT directly below—they view themselves as being at the center of a series of concentric circles, with the organization radiating outward. For them, as the case study in the next chapter details, the solution to the perpetual problem of the SMT doesn't lie in psychology; it lies in the adroit use of a custom-tailored portfolio of related teams. It is found not in a monolith but in a multiplicity.

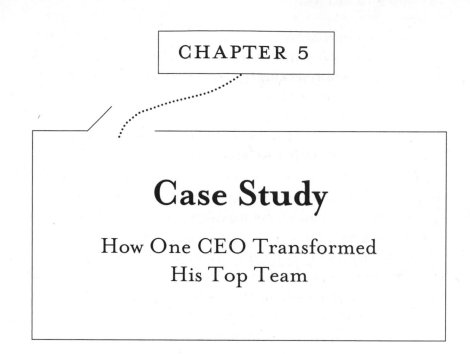

CHAPTER 5

Case Study

How One CEO Transformed His Top Team

Leaders who decide to look beyond the monolithic model of the Senior Management Team (SMT) have an opportunity to adopt a far more effective approach to management. Instead of seeing the Senior Management Team as the center of senior management decision making, they get the kind of support they need by creating and using a set of interrelated teams, one of which should be the SMT in a redefined, repurposed, and clear role. Some of these teams will be permanent; others will be created around a specific project or decision and then disbanded. Some will be official teams, fully documented on organization charts, process flows, and similar corporate blueprints. Others will be ad hoc—like kitchen cabinets. Some will be large; others may have only two or three members.

These teams provide the leader with a range of options. Which team is put into play will depend on the nature of the process, issue, or decision at hand. The leader can use a team appropriate for the particular purpose rather than trying to force-fit the SMT to an inappropriately broad range of situations.

One leader who has looked past the SMT monolith is Thomas J. Wilson, chairman, president, and CEO of The Allstate Corporation, who has reshaped the senior management structure of this $31 billion, 35,000-employee company. The case study in this chapter describes his thinking and experience, beginning with his original decision to move away from a Senior Management Team structure and then examining his implementation of a newly configured set of teams—an implementation that is still evolving.

The creation of this new management architecture was not something my firm was directly involved in. Although I have worked with Tom many times over the years, I came across the restructuring as it was in motion, in the course of doing the CEO interviews that provide the backbone of this book's content. Tom's willingness to share his story and his insights provides a realistic look into one of the many possibilities that a CEO has for configuring key teams. His story is not a generic best-practices model or a smoothed-over puff piece, but a highly specific, real-life example that presents how decisions really happen at Allstate. Clearly, the idea here is not that you should reproduce Tom's model in your own enterprise but instead learn from his experience and consider how this approach might be suitably adapted for your situation and preferences as a leader.

The Past as Prologue

Finding the combination of teams that works best for you requires not only acknowledging reality but delving into some history. In many organizations, team structures and processes have simply been handed on from one leader to another with little reflection by successors about whether that legacy really suits them.

The SMT structure Tom inherited when he became CEO had been created in 1995 by then CEO Jerry Choate. Although Choate was chairman and CEO, he wanted to maintain day-to-day oversight of the dominant Property and Casualty (P&C) side of Allstate's business, so he created a multilevel structure—an SMT that consisted of his direct reports plus a few key executives two levels down in the organization chart, like the heads of Claims and Distribution. By having the key P&C operational executives on the SMT alongside his direct reports, Choate was able to directly manage the most critical parts of the entire business from a single table, with the SMT incorporating his Operating Committee, and he could use the SMT structure to stay directly involved in the day-to-day management of 80 percent of the corporation's business.

Tom's immediate predecessor, Edward "Ed" Liddy, maintained Choate's structure during his tenure as CEO. But Liddy's style was to adopt more of a corporate approach, and he left most operational decisions to the presidents of the divisions. Liddy was also more of a kitchen cabinet CEO, whose style favored frequent one-on-one discussions with his subordinates and close advisers.

Under Liddy the SMT met regularly, primarily for communications reasons and to make sure the various parts of the organization were aligned on major issues and initiatives. The team's periodic offsite strategy meetings included discussions of high-level topics, but participants were well aware that major strategy decisions were being made by Liddy and his closest advisers.

Those in the know, including all the members of the SMT, realized that there was a kind of hub-and-spoke model at work. Liddy maintained strong personal relationships with many of his direct reports, especially chief investment officer Casey Sylla and general counsel Robert Pike and Pike's successor, Michael McCabe. Liddy also relied on several of his key board members to help guide him, most notably Ed Brennan, former chairman and CEO of Sears, Roebuck and Co.; James Denny, former vice chairman of Sears and Liddy's former boss at G. D. Searle; and W. James Farrell, chairman of Illinois Tool Works. Liddy's most frequent confidant was probably Tom—as Tom rotated through the roles of CFO, head of the life insurance business, head of the P&C business, and president. Ed Liddy would occasionally convene a small group to kick around ideas. Sometimes it was Ed, Tom, and John Carl, Tom's successor as CFO. Or Ed, Tom, John, and the heads of P&C, Life, and Investments.

Liddy's style as a classic kitchen cabinet CEO—primarily in a one-on-one, hub-and-spoke style with himself as the hub—was a departure from Choate's style of thrashing out a wide set of issues, operational and strategic, with the entire SMT gathered around the table. And so the SMT's role under Liddy shifted from a focus on operational decision making to an alignment and communications function.

Like many CEOs, Liddy tempered his natural instincts by deliberately introducing into his decision process trusted perspectives that differed from his own. But he didn't do this by bringing in the entire SMT and putting key strategic decisions on the table in front of the group as a whole.

Moving from a Single Top Team to Multiple Teams

When Tom Wilson became CEO, he already believed that the SMT structure he inherited wasn't going to provide the kind of support he needed to get Allstate where he knew it had to go. The kitchen cabinet approach was not his style either. "In general, I prefer a broader group of people in the conversation," Tom says. "Not so broad that it's unwieldy, but broader because I like to see the interplay between them. That's my personality, and I wanted an organization around me that supported that."

In addition, Tom puts great value on group decision making, despite its inherent difficulty. "Forcing the organization to decide builds sustainability," he says. "I didn't want to lead being only CEO-centric."

Ed Liddy structured the transition to Tom Wilson in a way that gave Tom the opportunity to build a team around the company's future needs and strategy and Tom's operating style. Shortly after his appointment as CEO was announced in October 2006, Tom told the Senior Management Team that the company needed to become more consumer-centric, requiring the organization to become faster and more flexible.

At the same time, Tom had to replace a number of the existing SMT members, some as a result of natural turnover and some in order to build more capabilities, eventually expanding the group from twelve to sixteen members. He also recognized that the multilevel structure that Jerry Choate had put in place required adjustment. "There's always a reluctance to let go of history," he explains. "It's like taking an engine apart. Are you sure you can put it back together again? What do you mess with and what do you leave intact? You have to protect all that makes you strong but have the courage to change that which will keep you from adapting to the future."

When working with other CEOs in such situations, I've sometimes found it helpful to use the analogy of a suit of clothes. I tell them that in the first six months or so after they become chief executive they're going to be walking around looking a little funny because they're trying to wear a suit that was created for someone else. At some point they will decide that they need a suit that is tailored for them. And other people, potentially including their predecessors, are likely to remark on this: "You replaced the gray three-piece chalk-stripe center vent with a blue two-button slim fit with European side vents? And you had a special pocket put in for your iPhone and another for your reading glasses?" And that new CEO is going to have to say, "It's not for you, it's for me. It's the suit I want to wear."

You have to be comfortable defending your custom-made suit, because it's made for you and nobody else. You've got to build a leadership and management structure around your idiosyncrasies and preferences, your strengths and weaknesses, and it's not going to look right to everyone. But it doesn't have to. It's your suit.

During his first few years as CEO, Tom gave himself time to think about the change that needed to happen—the suit he needed to meet his specific needs as chairman, president, and CEO of Allstate. It needed to be more than simply changing out some of the members of his leadership team, and he thought it was also going to require more than merely limiting SMT membership to a peer group of his direct reports. Eventually, he realized that to drive the change in Allstate he was looking for, he would have to change the way the company was managed at the top. "A lot of times people think an organization is a piece of paper with names in boxes and a bunch of lines on it," he says. "In reality an organization is all about what you do. It's everything—process and structure, teams, and clarity about governance. Otherwise, institutional memory does not bend. The rest of the organization has to change, starting from the inner circle and then broadening to the wider ones."

Tom's first decision was to break up the responsibilities of the SMT into a set of several teams. "There are some topics for which you want to have a big group and other topics for which you don't," he says. "Your team dynamic and your decision-making process have to be built around that."

He wanted small, more nimble teams, each focused on a specific issue or set of issues. "I wanted a different operating model," he says. "I didn't want to run it from one chair with twelve people sitting around me."

Team size was his first criterion in creating these teams. "You can't have a good robust dialogue with sixteen people. Six people can do that. But when you get a large group, like our SMT, some people just go to the meetings and they don't actively participate. With a smaller group, you're not going to let somebody get through a whole day sitting there taking notes, drinking coffee, and not mixing into the conversation. With a small group, everyone is active in the conversation but it's large enough so you get divergent opinions. We become stronger as a team because of the breadth of our differences, not the degree of similarity. A small group enables those differences to come out and supports constructive challanges."

Tom started with a blank slate when determining what groups would replace the SMT. "Any new structure involves a number of factors: the people—both their capabilities and their development needs—the strategy, the structure of the broader organization, and the particular needs of our industry."

He ended up with five committees, some of which already existed and some of which were new: the Operating Committee, the Strategy and Reinvention Committee, the Enterprise Talent Committee, the Enterprise Risk and Return Committee, and the Investments Committee. The Enterprise Risk and Return group and the Investments group are standing committees that are necessary because Allstate is in the insurance industry. They had already been in place, providing their specialist functions, and they were retained intact during the redesign process. In 2011, the functions of the previous SMT were replaced by the three new committees and a reconstituted Senior Management Team, now called the Senior Leadership Team, with, as mentioned, sixteen members, including Tom.

The cornerstone of the new structure is the five-member Operating Committee, consisting of Tom, his CFO, and the heads of Allstate's three major businesses. The team meets every two weeks and more often if necessary. Its mandate is to establish short-term priorities, coordinate operations, and talk about ethics and compliance. Three of the five members have their own Operating Committees below them, running their businesses.

The Operating Committee is just that—the core team that operates Allstate on a day-to-day basis. Its charter is very different from the charter of the previous SMT. It is a highly tactical group dealing with a broad range of operational issues. It sometimes considers the things the company should be working on and, in those instances, says Tom, functions as a kind of kitchen cabinet.

The Operating Committee is also the only group that doesn't start its meetings with an agenda, a tactic that reinforces the immediacy of the topics the group is meant to address and helps to build the capabilities of the executives on the team. The members start the meeting by naming the topics they want to talk about, then they prioritize them and work their way through them in a deliberately loose and open-ended way. With his Senior Leadership Team, Tom controls the agenda, but with the Operating Committee, he says, "It's their opportunity and their responsibility to ask questions of each other."

What Tom calls his "nonhierarchical and informal" approach to these meetings is partially driven by the extremely high level of the participants, but he also does it for purposes of development. "I need to create an organization that can run without me, and the only way to do that is if the most senior members of my team have the opportunity to step up," he says. "I'm going to run this team on a holistic basis in order to get them to build bridges and gain insights into other parts of the company. If for some reason I'm not able to run the company, then this team can do it. And it helps me develop succession options."

Whereas the Operating Committee has a near-term focus, the Strategy and Reinvention Committee occupies the other end of the spectrum—the long-term strategic success of Allstate. The core of this team is the five members of the Operating Committee. They are joined by the heads of Marketing, Technology, and Corporate Communications (who also heads Reinvention, Allstate's innovation initiative). The group is chaired by Don Civgin, Allstate's CFO, and Don has his senior vice president of Strategy and Business Development sit in on the group's meeting as staff. With a longer time horizon than the Operating Committee, the group is responsible for overseeing the development of corporate strategy, allocating capital, considering acquisitions and divestitures, leading reinvention efforts, and approving business unit strategies.

Why not just give these responsibilities to the Operating Committee? Because layering in the broad, corporate perspective with the specific expertise of Marketing, Technology, and Communications adds to the richness of the conversation. Why not add these three executives to the Operating Committee?

Because a five-person group lends itself to a different type of discussion than an eight-person group does. The Strategy and Reinvention Committee discussions—in a two-hour meeting every two weeks—have a different structure, tenor, time frame, pace, degree of formality, and set of outcomes. The meetings feel totally different from Operating Committee meetings, even though five-eighths of the membership is the same.

The Operating Committee is executional, tactical, immediate. The Strategy and Reinvention Committee is thoughtful and reflective, paced for the longer term. One manages. The other oversees and guides. They are two very different forums to which Tom can bring discussions and seek input on his major decisions. And both are smaller in size and more focused in purpose than their predecessor—the twelve-member, all-purpose Senior Management Team.

Neither of these two new committees includes all of Tom's direct reports. The only group that comes close to representing his staff is the Enterprise Talent Committee. It is responsible for cyclical personnel processes (ratings, compensation, and assignments), core processes such as succession planning, and strategic HR issues like the creation of the employee value proposition.

Operating the company. Overseeing the strategy. And ensuring the development of talent. All the functions that were formerly carried out by a single Senior Management Team are now allocated to three committees.

The Team That Sits Together Works Together

Beyond the establishment of these fixed committees, Tom took another major step—co-location. He moved the top twenty executives, a superset of the former SMT, and sat them together. Until early in 2011, F9 (the entire ninth floor of F building on the Allstate campus in Northbrook, Illinois) housed two office suites, a kitchen, and a conference room. With just two executives, two secretaries, and a receptionist, "it was like a funeral home," Tom says.

The SMT occupied F7 and F8. From the hallways on those floors, separate doorways opened to the office of each executive's secretary. Past the secretary's desk another door opened to the executive's office and an adjoining conference room. Everything was hushed, and the only interactions were scheduled meetings or the occasional greeting in the snack rooms or restrooms. As a result, the SMT members spent a lot of time in meetings taking care of items that Tom thought should have been resolved elsewhere. "I felt that we weren't operating enough as a collective team around each other, and we were substituting SMT meetings for bumping into each other," he says.

Today the scene differs dramatically. The seventh, eighth, and ninth floors have been gutted. F9 is now a floor of conference facilities that can be booked by anyone within Allstate. F7 and F8, now connected by an internal stairway, contain small glass-walled offices—all exactly the same size—for twenty executives. A number of conference rooms, also glass, are shared. The desks of the administrative assistants are just off the hallway, with no doors—they're working right in the open and are available to answer quick questions. There is a large, open kitchen, and chairs and couches in common areas for informal get-togethers. The offices now look much like the offices that Accenture built when I was a managing partner there—open, contemporary spaces designed to maximize frequent, informal interactions among the users, with less privacy, minimal formality, and no visible signs of hierarchy. Similar changes were made to the spaces for the other teams throughout the entire Allstate complex.

The new layout not only reflects the culture Tom is trying to instill at Allstate but is also a fundamental aspect of his management team redesign. Although the five standing committees have been established as focal points for specific types of conversations, Tom wanted spontaneous, free-flowing interactions taking place throughout the day. And executives are, in fact, dramatically increasing the number of their "have you got a minute?" and "let's work this out right now" sorts of conversations, taking advantage, as Tom envisioned, of a kind of support group beyond the groups that they lead—behaving differently and in a more collaborative fashion.

Co-location of the expanded set of executives on these two floors—the twelve former SMT members plus up to eight additional executives—also helped Tom deal with one downside of his new committee structure: what to do with the SMT members who weren't asked to sit on any of the five committees.

"When we made the changes some people were trying to figure out where they fit into the new structures," Tom says. "They wondered why they weren't on any committees." He had a ready response: they could attend any meeting they thought they needed to attend, keeping in mind that the purpose of the restructuring was to make sure leadership groups were small and effective.

His second response was to cite the ineffectiveness of the former SMT structure. He would ask the executives if they felt they'd had much input on the old team. When they said no, he asked if they felt the company was making much progress in the meetings. This would get another no. Then he would ask if the company should be moving faster in those meetings. When they said yes, he would say, "OK. That's why we're doing this."

Tom's third response, as the leader of Allstate who needed this structure to drive the company's success, was to stick to his guns:

> Sometimes people think of it as a democratic thing, but I wasn't elected. I don't need everyone around here to agree with me, as long as they respect me. I'd like them to like me, but not everything I do is going to make everyone happy.
>
> I think you might as well declare it. When you declare it, it makes it less personal in my own view. It's just a business decision. And they understand that, as opposed to thinking that I don't like them or I don't value their opinions because they don't get to talk about strategy. But while it's not a democracy, they do have to understand that they're valued.

The Senior Leadership Team (SLT) is more than an honorary group for the former SMT members. Tom sees the team as having a critical alignment focus. "It was clear that I moved decision making from the SMT to the committees. That was intentional on my part. The SMT used to have formal accountability for resource allocation and overall strategy, and those have moved. So the SLT has operational planning, coordination, and organizational alignment. Right now we're scheduled to have a monthly meeting, and go offsite a few times a year. My intention is for the SLT to meet rarely in formal meetings, and members of the SLT to meet constantly with each other, since we all sit together now."

The Operating Committee and the SLT are the only two groups without documented annual goals and objectives. They are forums, whereas the other four standing committees are tasked with specific outcomes through the SMART system of annual goal setting—SMART being an acronym for **S**pecific, **M**easurable, **A**ttainable, **R**elevant, and **T**imely.

This is the one area where Tom feels he should have moved more rapidly. "It has taken them some time to achieve focus and velocity in terms of what they're working on. The new structure would have taken hold faster if it had established hard, specific goals for the first year. It would have gotten things up and running faster."

The Operating Committee and the SLT provide Tom with two fluid forums for a variety of topics—a small group for rapid operational decisions and a large group for communications, alignment, and brainstorming. But there is one function of the former SMT that was intentionally not relocated—its role as catchall for the variety of minor issues and decisions that clutter the agendas of most leadership teams because those items seemingly have nowhere else to go.

When my firm is brought in to facilitate a strategy offsite for a new client, an offsite agenda is often already under development. Almost invariably, one of the most important meetings of the year has a third to half of its agenda already committed to a grab bag of miscellaneous topics. Forty-five minutes taken up here, an hour there. Everyone seems to think, "As long as the SMT is getting together, it's a good chance to review thus-and-so." And as I like to say, everyone seems to have hung an ornament on the Christmas tree. Given the broad representation offered by the typical SMT and that team's assumed role in not only important decisions but also *most* decisions, it's natural that a certain amount of organizational detritus gets caught up in its agendas.

Where will these issues go at Allstate? The important ones will find their way onto the agenda of one of the standing committees. Others may end up on Tom's desk. But the hope is, ideally, that many of them will be dealt with quickly and informally by the subset of senior management that needs to be involved. Or that they will be resolved at a lower level of the organization, never reaching F7 or F8. Without the magnet of the SMT as the be-all and end-all of decision making, these issues should, over time, find other, more appropriate, places to land. And that should free up significant amounts of the senior executives' time.

Tailoring the Structure to Suit Your Needs as a Leader

The first time I visited Allstate's renovated executive offices on the eighth floor of F building, Tom pointed out to me that all the offices were the same size. His office retained a great corner view, but as he pointed out, it was otherwise indistinguishable from the offices of the executives who worked for him. "Yes," I said, "but yours is the only one with a private conference room attached. All the others share conference rooms."

"You're right," he replied, "I have the only office that opens to a conference room, although there is a second door directly into the hallway and so it's not mine to use exclusively. But let me explain why I did that." Tom said that he wanted everyone's office to be the same size so that the members of the Senior Leadership Team would feel like peers, regardless of who reports to whom on the organization chart. And, he said, he also did it out of consideration for his eventual successor. "The next CEO may not think like me. My office is pretty small for the head of a corporation this size. So I wanted to give the next person an option. By taking down one wall, the new occupant of the office can double the personal space and have a more typically sized CEO corner office without going through the cost of another major renovation."

Just as Tom inherited a structure, both physical and organizational, that didn't fit him, the next CEO might find Tom's structure not right for him or her. Tom Wilson took Allstate's monolithic Senior Management Team structure, originally created by his predecessor's predecessor, and dismantled it, replacing it with a new top-management organization tailored to his needs. The next CEO might need to do something similar.

As I said at the outset of this chapter, there is no one best way. Says Tom, "Ed Brennan [the late chairman and CEO of Sears, Roebuck and Co.] told me that an organization structure should be based on who you are—what your personality is as a leader. I used to think that was wrong, but now I realize that's the only way an organization can function."

Tom Wilson tailored a suit to his personality and to running a particular company, following a specific strategy, at a given point in time. "Harnessing the hearts, minds, and passions of the individuals who make up Allstate is more important to success than some ideal team structure," he says. "That is one thing that Jerry, Ed, and I have been entirely consistent about—the power of the individual. The team structure is really a form for organizing, aligning, and leveraging diverse individual talent towards the company's goals under a particular leadership style."

And, for now, Tom's suit fits that purpose well.

Fortunately, even though each custom-tailored suit is unique in many ways, all suits also share some characteristics. Two arms. Two legs. Buttons on the jacket. Pockets on the trousers. So even though there is no one best practice for structuring an organization to replace the existing monolithic model of the Senior Management Team, there are some best practices and principles—plural, like the teams themselves—that can guide you in your thinking about how to lead through a system of interrelated teams. These best practices are the subject of the next chapter.

CHAPTER 6

Best Practices

Design an Organization That Delivers the Outcomes You Need

Unless you are an astronaut or a brain surgeon or you pursue some other similarly self-explanatory profession, you have likely had a child ask you, "What do you do?" And if you said that you were a corporate executive, you were probably asked the question a second time, but with an added emphasis: "But what do you *do?*" In candid moments, many executives would confess, "Mostly, I go to meetings."

Various studies over the years have found that the average executive spends anywhere from 30 to 50 percent of his or her working hours in meetings and that as much as a third of that time is unproductive. My experience is that these estimates are on the low side, especially as you get toward the top of an organization. In organizations where standing committees proliferate and executives jockey for membership in as many high-profile groups as possible, meetings consume more and more time. And although there is lots of activity, there is too little action. Instead there is inertia, bureaucracy, people stretched way too thin to be fully effective, and a culture that equates *busy* with *important*.

The solution for many companies is to learn how to have more effective meetings. There's nothing wrong with having more effective meetings—one of the things I do for a living is facilitate strategy offsites. But why optimize a meeting that's about the wrong things, with the wrong people, at the wrong time, or the meetings of a team that shouldn't exist in the first place? Executives do sometimes question why a meeting is happening or if the right people are there or whether the dynamics are conducive to good teamwork, but they rarely question the rationale for the existence of the team in the first place.

CEOs can cut through this inefficiency by explicitly putting in place a more flexible and fluid portfolio approach that focuses on what teams are best for what tasks, not on issues of representation and hierarchy. *Flexible* and *fluid* are the keys. I am emphatically *not* proposing replacing a current set of standing teams and committees with an alternative set of standing teams and committees—that is simply reshuffling the organizational deck. In the reengineering wave in the 1990s, I worked with a number of organizations undergoing massive transformation programs. Although much good came from these efforts, in my view they often replaced one rigid management structure with another. They got a better machine, but what I am proposing here will result not in a highly formal structure but in an organic, flexible, and situational approach.

In laying out best practices, I will be arguing for eliminating as many permanent groups and committees as is feasible and replacing them with objectives-based teams. This drives you away from management by the organization chart and toward an outcomes-based approach to team management. This simply means that in any situation calling for the involvement of a team, a leader should start not with the group that the organization chart or the committee structure implies should be engaged but with the outcome that he or she is seeking. Then the leader can use or create the right team to supply that outcome—whether the team is formal, informal, permanent, or temporary. Instead of trying to run a machine, with its bias for process, hierarchy, and structure, the boss operates in a fluid reality, with a bias for action and a relentless focus on outcomes.

Process, hierarchy, and structure do not disappear—this is not the familiar and futile call for organizational democracy. But process, hierarchy, and structure aren't the primary determinants of how the boss uses teams—desired outcomes are. Who goes into the room depends on what the boss wants to come out of the room.

The Three Centers of Gravity

Adopting these best practices doesn't require the CEO to start with a blank sheet of paper and completely redraw the organization chart or rethink every team and committee. The starting point is a consideration of three teams already in existence in most organizations: the kitchen cabinet, the senior management team (SMT), and the larger all-officers group (or the SMT plus direct reports or some similar configuration). Each of these teams, by virtue of its size and composition, is better at producing some kinds of outcomes than others.

Kitchen Cabinet

Kitchen cabinets—unnamed, unofficial advisory groups—are almost always small, sometimes as small as one other person besides the CEO. Small groups are much better for considering decisions than larger groups, which, as we've seen, may find decision making almost impossible.

Composition—the precise membership of this group at a given time—is equally important. The bona fides of participants can take a variety of forms. One person may be in the room because he is the CEO's Bobby Kennedy—the adviser the boss trusts most. Another may have special knowledge of the issue at hand—for example, a chief financial officer (CFO) will have insights in regard to a possible acquisition. Someone else may be there because she has a breadth and depth of knowledge comparable to the CEO's and sees the world similarly. Another may be there because he can be relied on to push back relentlessly and question the CEO's assumptions.

Says Ellyn McColgan, former president and chief operating officer of Morgan Stanley Global Wealth Management Group: "There are the ones you rely on because you respect their opinion, or the ones you have known the longest, and the ones who are willing to be contrarian and let you hear something you might not want to know. These are the people who would never lie to me, who would stop me from making a mistake, who would never withhold information from me. I always need someone close to me who will tell me when I'm in danger of going off the rails."

Further, the composition can change—and often should change—depending on the issue. Although most kitchen cabinets usually include the CFO, there may be no reason to have this officer present for every nonfinancial decision. There may also be instances in which the CEO seeks counsel from trusted peers outside the organization. The CEO may, in effect, have several kitchen cabinets.

Says Sean Moriarty, former CEO of Ticketmaster, "The danger of trying to think through problems exclusively with people inside the company is that it can lead unintentionally to groupthink. As much as you'd like to say that you can get perspective through the other members of your team, the reality is that they're living inside the organization and you spend a lot of time together. There are a half a dozen people that I talk to regularly. They're all business professionals, but they're also close friends I trust and who know me—who provide the professional and the personal context for the conversation. That's my real kitchen cabinet."

Just as they might flex any team, some CEOs vary the composition of their kitchen cabinets. But whether kitchen cabinets are fixed or fluid, they all have one thing in common—they never have a name.

Referring to the kitchen cabinet only informally—as, say, "Ed and Ted and Mary"—instead of giving it a formal structural identity and an official name, does more than preserve the option of a fluid membership. It also severely limits, or eliminates, lobbying by any individual for inclusion in the group or its discussions.

Let's say a CEO gives her kitchen cabinet a name and an official box on the organization chart. As soon as the announcement goes out, this CEO will have people banging on her door, asking to be admitted to the group solely on the basis of the positions they hold—the legislative mentality in action. "If you're going to be talking about plant expansion in new markets" one caller will say, "how can you not have Operations in the room?" Soon there's another knock on the door: "Hey, if you're getting together for a strategy discussion, shouldn't you include Marketing?" Pretty soon, the whole SMT is attending the meetings, or at least lobbying for entry.

If the group has no name, lobbying for inclusion becomes harder, and there's therefore much less of it. It's easy to ask, "Why shouldn't Marketing have a seat at the table for these XYZ Committee discussions?" It's much more challenging to say to the CEO, "The next time you get Ted and Mary together to talk about a big decision, you should have me in the room."

As Ellyn McColgan says of the kitchen cabinet, "Its power lies in its being unofficial. You can choose to include whoever you want—it's bureaucracy free."

The small size and fluid, handpicked composition of the kitchen cabinet also help to ensure the candor required for a full airing of the issues and the freedom to kick around ideas in the way only intimate colleagues can. Floating trial balloons and shooting them down can be a messy process, one that can unnecessarily stir up concerns in larger groups like the SMT, where some participants might spot issues that would affect them in a what-if scenario. CEOs benefit greatly from the advice and pushback of these small, trusted groups who speak freely and keep confidences.

Senior Management Team

A medium-sized group, providing it is representative of the company, is the ideal venue for alignment. Such a group can get all the relevant parts of the organization coordinated and working together to achieve broad general objectives. In contrast, the members of a small group, such as a kitchen cabinet, may work well together, but because they don't represent all parts of the organization they cannot fully drive alignment. And it's difficult for a larger body, such as an all-officers group, typically somewhat cumbersome and not meeting frequently, to be the focal point of alignment.

The SMT, with its typical eight to fourteen members, representing all the major functions and domains of the business, is ideally positioned to focus on alignment. And not just on alignment in general but, by virtue of its members' status as staff to the CEO, alignment around three of any organization's most critical issues: vision, resource allocation, and execution.

All-Officers or Similar Large Group

A group somewhat larger than the SMT is ideal for generating ideas, uncovering options, implementing initiatives, and bringing diverse perspectives and creativity to difficult issues. In the midst of a strategy formulation process, for example, this group may be convened to brainstorm or to help generate ideas for what may be a smaller team directing the overall effort. Kitchen cabinets are too small to undertake this task, and SMTs, although larger and more diverse than kitchen cabinets, are still too small to guarantee that the broadest possible range of options will surface.

The composition of this group, like the composition of the kitchen cabinet, may vary according to the circumstances. It may be an all-officers group at times, or as at Allstate, it may be a broadened Senior Leadership Team, or it may be some combination of the SMT, selected direct reports, and high-potential individuals from further down in the organization.

No one of these three groups is necessarily superior to the others. The waste and inefficiency comes when a group is asked to perform tasks for which it is not well suited. This happens most often with the SMT, which is not surprising, given the widely shared assumptions about its status as the all-purpose group running the company and the fact that among these three major, ready-to-hand teams it's the only one that isn't flexed for maximum relevance and effectiveness.

It's important to note that the tasks mentioned here aren't the only things that these naturally occurring teams are good at—all three are adaptable to a variety of purposes. For example, both the SMT and the larger groups can, by virtue of their representativeness, be good vehicles for communication to the entire organization, and CEOs frequently use them for that purpose. But for three of the most critical types of tasks that teams near the top of an organization need to accomplish, these are the best teams for accomplishing them: counseling the boss on major decisions in the case of kitchen cabinets, alignment in the case of the SMT, and idea generation and implementation in the case of the larger groups.

In this approach there is no longer one presumed center of gravity—the SMT—but three. A CEO who needs to make and validate a major decision will gravitate to a kitchen cabinet, whose precise composition may depend on the nature of the decision. A CEO who wants to maximize alignment around the general direction of the company or a course of action will turn naturally to the SMT. For brainstorming, identifying obstacles, and mobilizing for implementation, a larger group will be clearly best.

Around and beyond these three centers of gravity, numerous other teams may exist or need to be created. Some of these teams will be permanent, depending on the nature of the industry or the business. For example, companies in the financial services industry usually need a standing Risk Management Committee. Pharmaceutical companies may have permanent Compliance Committees; utility companies may have Capacity Management Teams, and so on. In addition there may be standing special-purpose teams for issues like acquisitions and strategy.

A company's leaders will also have a team for each of the many initiatives that are usually under way in any organization. The focus here is on strategic initiatives—those high-impact, cross-functional projects occurring outside the realm of business as usual and requiring sponsorship, guidance, or support from the top of an organization. Unlike standing committees, initiative teams typically have a finite life span and are oriented toward a specific outcome: enter a new market, develop a strategy, integrate an acquisition, or respond to a competitor's new product, for example.

Whether the CEO interacts with, or is even aware of, any given initiative team depends on the importance of the initiative. In the case of a major strategic initiative the CEO may play a significant role in appointing the team's leader and its key members and may occasionally sit in on its meetings. In other cases the CEO may get involved only when an initiative is going poorly. As one CEO told me, "I always want to stay in touch with these teams so, if necessary, I know whose throat to choke."

Flexing in Five Dimensions

Leaders can increase the likelihood that they will get the outcomes they are seeking by thoughtfully flexing teams along five critical dimensions: number, size, composition, issue ownership, and timing. Some best practices for each of these dimensions are described in the following sections.

The Number of Teams Should Be No More Than Absolutely Necessary to Achieve Desired Outcomes. This is so self-evidently true that I hesitate to mention it. But in my experience most organizations have far too many standing committees, with far too many regularly scheduled meetings. It's not surprising that many executives spend almost half of their working lives in meetings. As one CEO says, "Standing committees waste tons of time. In a world where you're out there with things that need to get done every day and, on top of that, you then have to try to generate the work to justify a committee meeting—that always feels to me counterproductive and forced." Or as my late friend and mentor Mike Norman used to say, "You can go to meetings or you can go to work."

In addition to being enormous time wasters, says former Ticketmaster CEO Sean Moriarty, standing committees are usually unprepared and lack the resources to deal with the unpredictable events that inevitably arise, even in the course of a single year. In his view the best way to attack unexpected events is through project-based teams: "When these things come up you want to be able to solve them and then get your resources applied to your plan again as quickly as you can. There's no way to do that through a standing committee because you have no idea which people are going to be available and capable of solving the situations that you didn't see coming."

The vigilant CEO will challenge the existence of every standing committee—Does this group really need to exist in perpetuity? Does it really need to meet regularly? Is this a productive use of the time of highly compensated executives?

Beware of the natural bias in favor of keeping standing committees simply because they have existed for a long time or because it's difficult to imagine not having a permanent group to deal with a certain issue. As noted, some industries and business models require some standing committees, but many other standing committees are dispensable if the CEO is willing to be aggressive in questioning their existence and creative in finding alternatives to fulfilling whatever essential functions they do provide.

Even when you have a perennial issue, you don't necessarily need a standing committee for it. One CEO I worked with, instead of maintaining a permanent capability for formulating strategy, addressed strategy issues through a series of projects run out of the Office of the CEO. He would create ad hoc teams composed of members whose competencies were relevant for a particular aspect of the company's situation and have those high-potential executives engage in a set of structured strategy conversations with his Executive Committee. He was free to compose each new project team according to his perception of specific company needs, building teams based on the people he wanted to involve and not necessarily the positions those people held at the time.

One of the strongest contributors to one corporate vision project this CEO put together was an attorney in the organization's regulatory and compliance area. His participation in this initiative was a significant developmental step in a number of ways. He helped put together a truly great piece of strategy work and developed his own skills as a result. In the process the Executive Committee got a good look at his ability to operate in a context different from his usual area. Four years later, he became general manager of one of the most promising of the company's growth platforms. Had there been a standing Strategy Committee, he would not have been a participant in the project to set a strategic direction.

Once the strategic direction had been finalized and approved by the board, the CEO dismantled the entire project apparatus. To his mind, creating vision isn't an ongoing process. It's something done for four to six months every three to five years using a combination of outside consultants, built-to-purpose initiative teams, his Executive Committee, and his board.

Size Should Be Determined by the Desired Outcome at Each Stage of a Conversation. As we've seen with the three naturally occurring teams—the kitchen cabinet, the SMT, and the all-officers group—the size of a group makes it better at some things than others. The same principle should be applied to all teams. If the desired outcome is a decision, keep the team small. If alignment is the goal, a medium-sized, representative group is usually best. For generating ideas or implementation, go bigger.

Remember, however, that different outcomes may be desired at different points in a conversation that takes place over time. A team charged with developing a new Internet strategy may need to brainstorm at some point fairly early in the conversation. The team might therefore be expanded from the core group, becoming much larger so that a sufficient number of potentially attractive options can emerge from the wide variety of perspectives in the room. The brainstorming process might unfold over one meeting or many, but until that particular outcome is achieved, the larger group is the team. To finish the work and recommend a course of action, the team should probably revert to a smaller core group. For aligning the organization around the course of action, the core group can expand again until it is representative of all the parts of the organization that will need to pull together.

The analogy I like to use is that this is like playing an accordion. If you need to make decisions, you squeeze down to a small-sized group. If you want creativity and brainstorming, lots of options, and lots of different eyes exploring the different aspects of something, then you open up to a wide group.

Although flexing team size may seem self-evidently sensible, many organizations hamstring themselves at the outset of a task by locking in a fixed team that is too large. The impulse is to try to make every team fully representative, by function, geography, division, or some combination of these factors. Often, too, individuals will lobby to be on various teams because they regard membership as prestigious or career enhancing. As Sean Moriarty says, "Your prestige in the company is determined by how many meetings you attend and at what level."

Both of those tendencies can often be seen in action in a roomful of people doing RACI charting (as described in Chapter Three, this process identifies the team **R**esponsible for doing a particular piece of work, the individual **A**ccountable for seeing that the work is done, the individuals or groups who should be **C**onsulted for their opinions about the work, and the individuals or groups who should be **I**nformed as the work takes place). There are keywords that go along with each RACI element. For Accountable, the keyword is *one*—only one person can be ultimately accountable for the outcome. For Responsible, the keyword is *team*—this is the core team that's going to do the work. For Consulted, it's *before*—particular people or groups expect to be consulted before the team makes any major recommendations that might affect them or their areas. And for Informed, it's *after*—the team should go ahead and do its work, and it's all right to inform certain people and groups afterward about what it has come up with.

Whenever I facilitate RACI charting, the first pass always ends up with far too many people insisting that they or someone from their organization should be listed as Responsible. If this is an important initiative, the logic goes, either I or someone from my group ought to be on the team. So geographies get added. And functional areas. Marketing wants to have someone sit in, and of course Finance should be represented in case there's an income statement impact. HR should be there, because personnel-related issues are sure to arise. In no time, every team has a dozen or more members. Few people initially want to be relegated to the status of Consulted or Informed. Their motives—personal ambition and the desire for representation—are understandable, but the result is that most teams start too large. At the outset of team formation, it's well to remember Amazon.com founder Jeff Bezos's rule of thumb about team size: any working team that can't be fed with just two pizzas is too big.[1]

Composition Should Be Determined by the Nature of the Issue at Each Stage of the Conversation. Just as teams can be flexed in size depending on the desired outcome at any given point, they can be flexed in composition, understood as the kinds of expertise different individuals bring to the conversation. Different kinds of expertise may be needed at different points in an ongoing, important discussion, but there is no reason to bring that expertise on board for the full conversation; it can be added during the specific period of time it is needed in the discussion.

For example, a strategy project might include a work stream requiring the analysis of various ways to segment a given market. When it is known at the outset that segmentation might be involved, the natural tendency is to put a Marketing representative on the team for the duration. But the analysis might be occurring only during a few weeks of a six-month project and might affect only one aspect of a complex strategic analysis. There's no reason for the Marketing head to be a permanent member of the group, or even to assign a Marketing staffer to sit in on the weekly project meetings for half a year. It's better to offer subject matter expertise on an as-needed basis and let a smaller core team get on with its work.

Composition is of course inextricably related to size. If you add and subtract individuals according to the current need for their expertise, the size of the team changes. Nevertheless, size and composition are not identical and shouldn't be confused, especially as both attributes are being flexed over the course of a conversation. At any point you should be able to say: "I want *this many* people in the room because I want a particular kind of outcome right now. I have *these particular individuals* in the room because they understand the issue we're discussing right now." Size and composition may be interdependent, but they are separate considerations, and the careful CEO will keep the distinction in mind when creating a team.

Issue Ownership Should Be Determined by the Requirements of the Conversation, Not by a Charter. There is no iron rule that says a particular team has to handle an issue from beginning to end. Different points in the conversation may require the participation of different teams. For example, discussion of a potential acquisition may start in a business development group, move to a kitchen cabinet, go from there to an acquisition team for study and due diligence, be handed off to the SMT for review, and finally go back to the kitchen cabinet, where the CEO then makes a decision. After the deal is consummated the CEO might bring it to the all-officers group to enlist the members' buy-in and involvement in communications and integration rollout planning; at which point a series of task forces might be established to bring the two companies together and realize their synergistic potential.

Although this kind of fluid internal movement is how most companies actually work, it's rarely overtly planned, deliberately implemented, or clearly spelled out in advance. Under those circumstances even the most linear movement can be interpreted by some managers and executives as an initiative rattling around inside a company, with the linkages, movement, and especially the objectives at each stage of the process remaining ambiguous.

The Timing of the Parts of a Task Should Accelerate the Tempo of the Business. In some cases the timing of a team's work will be tied to the budget cycle. In some cases it will be dictated by an urgent need—come up with a new market strategy by the next board meeting. But in all cases timing is tied to outcome and objectives, so the team is faced with not just a question of *what* but also of *by when*. The task is to orchestrate all of the time frames so that they are in harmony and—most important—to accelerate their work so that the entire business is faster, more nimble, responsive, and proactive.

Having clearly timed objectives and outcomes has an additional virtue: initiatives, projects, and their associated teams might actually end. When sunset provisions are implicit in them, efforts eventually get starved for resources, shrink, and disappear, thereby freeing up much needed resources for the next initiative opportunity.

The Portfolio and the Payoff

With an unbounded ability to define an organization's universe of teams and with principles for leveraging those teams' number, size, composition, issue ownership, and timing, the CEO has a powerful set of tools for getting the most out of the organization. There is no defaulting to an approach that is vaguely based on the organization chart, ill-defined notions of representativeness, and an unexamined acceptance of permanent structures. Instead, the CEO molds a portfolio of teams based on desired outcomes and what each team does best. The portfolio typically includes the three naturally occurring teams, select standing committees, and a carefully managed and appropriately changing group of task-specific initiative teams with the right members, milestones, metrics, work plans, allocated resources, and end points. Guided by the principle of managing teams for outcomes and armed with the ability to flex the portfolio as well as the key dimensions of individual teams, the CEO can cut incisively through the clutter, the inaction, and the sheer management sclerosis that afflicts almost every organization to some degree or another. The payoff is significant:

- **The reality of the kitchen cabinet gains legitimacy.** Acknowledging the use and desirability of kitchen cabinets puts the actual role of the SMT into a more realistic context, clarifies where decisions are actually made, and allows the organization to dispense with useless efforts at SMT team building.
- **Teams get better outcomes, faster.** Optimized by size, composition, issue ownership, and timing to achieve desired outcomes, teams are better equipped to address the issues they face and to do so faster.

- **The organization gains increased velocity and agility.** The combination of the adroit use of the portfolio as a whole, the optimal configuration of individual teams, and the determination to manage teams toward outcomes enables the organization to purposefully become a responsive, evolving organism—instead of a self-perpetuating machine whose wheels grind slowly.

- **The SMT is freed to do what it does best.** Far from being reduced in importance, the SMT is able to focus on the thing it does best: align the organization in such critical areas as vision, allocation of resources, and execution (activities explored in detail in Part Two of this book).

- **CEOs get organizations that fit their personal approach to leading.** All the CEOs I've worked with balance, in varying proportions, both a strong bias for action and a need for the best possible input and advice. There is no ideal mixture and therefore no one ideal organizational design for embodying someone's approach to leadership. The flexible management of a portfolio of teams enables individual CEOs to create organizations tailored to their unique preferences. Instead of having to flex their personalities, as the behavioralists advise, they can do something far easier and more productive—flex the organization.

The ability to lead teams ranks high on almost everyone's list of leadership competencies. But there is rarely any mention of the ability to *use* teams. Yet CEOs get more leverage from using teams than from sitting at the head of the table leading them. CEOs who are adept at using the many teams at their disposal achieve better outcomes, field teams that waste less time and talent, deploy the right people against the right issues, and help the enterprise to free itself from the tyranny of the organization chart. And they can say goodbye to the shrinks and behavioralists sniffing out dysfunction and urging leaders to improve themselves or to democratize accountability. Why? Because the organization knows the real secret of team effectiveness: what makes teams effective is a CEO who knows how to use them to achieve their desired outcomes.

That's great leadership.

Note

1. Alan Deutschman, "Inside the Mind of Jeff Bezos," *Fast Company* (August 1, 2004).

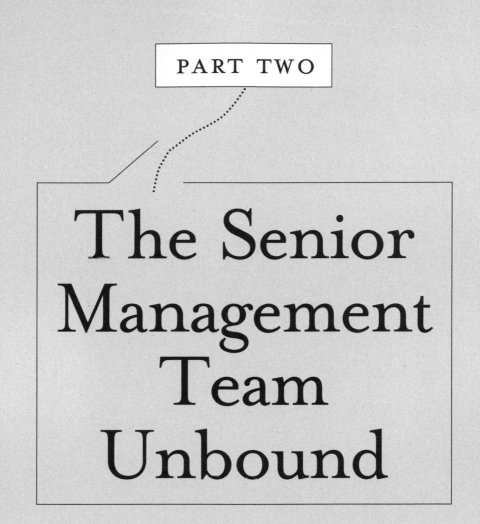

PART TWO

The Senior Management Team Unbound

Engage the Senior Management Team in Three Critical Conversations No Other Team Can Have

No other team in an organization combines the seniority, representativeness, collective wisdom, experience, and competence of the senior management team (SMT). But those extraordinary characteristics rest on a very ordinary foundation—team members' status as staff to the boss.

Several of the CEOs I engaged in the research for this book have made a point of renaming their executive committees simply "X's Staff." At the American Red Cross, for example, CEO Gail McGovern's top team is known as "Gail's direct reports." The thinking of these leaders is that every boss has a staff—this one just happens to be mine. The team members deal with high-level issues because they're high-level executives, but ultimately they're just another group of executives who have individual responsibilities for running a piece of the business and who periodically come together in support of the executive whose staff they form.

When the behavioralists put forward their various models of top teams, the SMT's basic identity as the staff for the executive at the head of the table often gets lost in an overemphasis on the group's unique status. Acting as staff to the top leader is no small thing. But it shouldn't automatically imply that the SMT, an advisory body, should also be given extraordinary power as a decision-making body, beyond the power of any other staff group. I can't think of a case where an executive has been put in charge of a division or function and her boss has said, "Mary, I'm putting you in charge of the Industrial Division. I want you and your team to make good decisions together—I'm counting on your group to run the business well, and I'm holding the group accountable for the outcome." It's Mary, not the group, who has accountability, and she has her staff to help her achieve her objectives. Nobody would make the staff the decision-making entity—Mary decides. Why is it that in the entire universe of staffs there is one staff—the CEO's staff—where the role is expected to shift from helping the boss make good decisions to making decisions as a group?

As one executive put it, "I changed their name from the Executive Committee to the President's Staff because I wanted people to stop treating them like gods." Once the SMT has been demythologized, then its members' seniority, their fully representative nature, their collective abilities, and the fact that they are also staff to the accountable executive can be used to best advantage.

Liberating the SMT from the illusion of being a decision-making body opens up the potential for the team to take on a more important role than ever. There is a whole spectrum of activities at which senior management teams excel—activities through which they can make a far bigger contribution to the success of the organization than by nominally approving business cases or dealing with myriad minor issues that have no other home.

As the most senior team, with all the key components of the organization simultaneously represented around the table, the SMT of course has an ongoing role to play in the day-to-day coordination of the business. As with any staff, providing ongoing, cross-functional oversight arises as a natural purpose of such a group. In fact, at many companies, operational coordination is the primary role of the leader's staff. But beyond this familiar operational role, the SMT has the potential to shine at several extremely important strategic tasks, the outcomes of which can profoundly affect the performance of the entire organization. These critical tasks are

- Developing a shared view of where the organization needs to go and why
- Managing a prioritized set of strategic initiatives designed to get there
- Managing dependencies within and among initiatives to ensure their success

In other words, these tasks concern vision, allocation of resources, and execution—three of the most critical responsibilities of top leadership.

Most leaders and their SMTs would likely say that they do in fact address all three of these issues. But in my experience, they are mostly engaged in an ongoing dialogue about running the business, consistent with their operational role. And they probably spend a few days a year at an offsite to consider higher-level issues of strategy. But those two-day meetings typically include half a day devoted to team building and the like, half a day spent on minor agenda items that they're dealing with because they happen to be together, and then maybe one day is available for a brief trip up to the 10,000-foot level of strategy.

In their regular weekly, biweekly, or monthly meetings their conversations around strategic issues are often limited as well. Slashing a few initiatives in a budget process or handling execution bottlenecks after they occur does not get the SMT working at the level that it could. Nor do the unsystematic conversations that occur when a business case lands on the meeting agenda. Even premeeting wiring—the seeking of buy-in for such cases from various members of the team before they meet on the issue—which is presumed to achieve alignment in advance, is essentially a one-off occurrence, with limited value for seeing the bigger strategic picture.

Fully leveraging the extraordinary potential of the SMT is best done through ongoing, structured conversations carried on by the boss and the senior team members. By *structured conversation* I don't mean a meeting agenda, a set of meeting objectives, or the illusion of structure created by PowerPoint templates. Agendas and objectives are of course important for almost any meeting, but the structured conversations I'm talking about have some unique features:

- They build structure into the discussion of the substance of the issues through frameworks that advance the conversation.
- They employ mechanisms that promote candor while defusing politically sensitive issues endemic to SMTs.
- They become part of the rhythm of the business—scheduled, planned, and executed at intervals throughout the year and with expected milestones.

It is these kinds of regular, formal, probing conversations about the team's view of the world, the allocation of resources, and the execution of initiatives that the boss and the SMT should be having. In my experience, these conversations can dramatically boost the team's contribution to the business and enable the CEO to make the most of the unique capabilities and perspectives of the SMT. Most important, they offer these invaluable advantages:

- **Structured conversations generate genuine insight and engagement.** The higher expectations, higher stakes, and unique nature of the three critical discussions leaders and SMTs should have require something more than the routine give-and-take of regular SMT meetings. Systematically structured conversations produce far more constructive outcomes than the approaches that confuse creativity with formlessness. Structured, however, doesn't mean stage managed. Unlike the nodding through of business cases, these conversations should be designed to induce engagement at the rational, political, and emotional levels. The issues are too important to be glossed over. As the single piece of paper with which Buffalo-based food company Rich Products launched one such a discussion said: "When friends argue, truth happens."[1]

- **Genuine engagement drives genuine alignment.** Alignment crucially bridges strategy and execution. It should not be confused with consensus. Alignment means that everyone, even individuals who are unhappy with an outcome, has agreed to do certain things. Consensus can sometimes describe an outcome with which everyone can live because conflict has been glossed over. Real alignment comes from the sweat equity earned during a conversation in which members of the team have been deeply engaged. Genuinely aligning an executive team around where the company needs to go, the initiatives that will take them there, and the dependencies within and among initiatives creates a far greater likelihood that strategies will be executed effectively.

- **The team feels empowered.** The importance of discussing the future of the company provides the SMT with a manifestly high purpose. They may no longer be the perceived epicenter of strategic decision making, but they are crafting the future strategic direction for the enterprise. These high-level, critical conversations, at one or two removes from the day-to-day operation of the business, enable team members not only to make substantive contributions to the company but also to feel that they are making such contributions.

- **The company takes control of its destiny.** Companies frequently call in consultants to develop their strategies. But
  it really should be up to the management team to figure out
  the solutions to the organization's issues of direction, priorities, and execution. Any CEO or SMT that turns those issues
  entirely over to consultants has abdicated a major responsibility of running the company.

What do these conversations look like? Chapter Eight will
answer that question with regard to developing a common
view of the world, Chapter Nine will attempt to do the same
for prioritizing and integrating initiatives, and Chapter Ten
will address managing dependencies. My purpose is not to give
you a how-to manual but a why-to and a what-to guide—why
your SMT should be having these conversations and what they
should be talking about. Few things are more important, few
conversations are more energizing, and in my experience, no
SMT exists that wouldn't welcome this critical strategic role.

Note

1. Bob Frisch and Logan Chandler, "Off-Sites That Work,"
   Harvard Business Review (June 2006), p. 121.

CHAPTER 8

Align the Senior Management Team Around a Common View of the World

The subject of vision makes some executives uneasy. It's not hard to understand why. Many people view corporate vision as akin to Moses descending from Mount Sinai with the revealed truth—a prophetic moment of blinding insight (coming from either the CEO or a McKinsey project team) that will lead the enterprise to some strategic promised land. Others see vision as stirring slogans that will fill the parking lots early and inspire employees to new levels of achievement. Pessimists may view a corporate vision as betting the company on some highly speculative view of the future or as a collection of generalities or platitudes containing too few details to have any real value.

When offsites are announced with vision on the agenda, the reaction is usually fifty-fifty. Half the attendees say, "Great. We could use a clear sense of where we're headed." The other half say sarcastically, "Great. Just what we need. Another day of meaningless wordsmithing."

A good starting point for making conversations about vision meaningful and relevant to a group like the Senior Management Team (SMT) is to pursue a deliberately pedestrian definition of vision by asking these questions: What is the next set of opportunities this company is going to pursue, and what are the capabilities that will lead us to realize those opportunities successfully? Arriving at the answers that will form the vision involves

- Developing a common view of changes in the external world
- Understanding the organization's existing capabilities for pursuing the opportunities that those changes will create and determining what new capabilities and assets will be needed in the future
- Defining the boundaries of the current business that will need to be modified or removed in order to pursue these specific opportunities

Once the vision has been established, the tools to operationalize it—initiatives, priorities, metrics—can be put into place. But the key is to first make sure that the SMT understands where the company is headed, why that direction makes sense, and what it will need to get there. Many failures of vision can be traced back to a failure to define and communicate one or more of those key understandings. Expressing the vision in deliberately pedestrian terms—opportunities, capabilities, and boundaries—makes the process highly accessible to the entire team, even if its members don't see themselves as particularly visionary.

Your executive team members can reach a mutual understanding about the world they are operating in and the opportunities, capabilities, and assets they have—or will need—to succeed in it. Developing a vision is no more, and no less, than the SMT building and articulating a common view of the future.

The Starting Point: Aligning Around Trends

Gaps between the ways individual members of an SMT view the world can be dramatic. But what is truly astonishing is not that they disagree; it's that they often don't even know that they disagree. Why? In many cases it's because they've never discussed it.

Some years ago I was working with a large, non-U.S. carpet manufacturer. The primary determinant of demand in the carpet industry is construction of new homes. At the time, new home construction in the company's domestic market was in a trough—that much everyone agreed on. But the head of Sales and the head of Operations disagreed on just about everything else. It seemed that whenever a large capital project was discussed, they were consistently on opposite sides of the issue.

In order to bring order out of conversational chaos, I scheduled a few hours for the SMT members to discuss their basic assumptions about the company's competitors and markets. Fact books containing internal, external, and trend data were distributed to the attendees. Within the first hour of the meeting a striking disparity of outlook emerged. It turned out that the head of Sales was firmly convinced that the company's home market was going to rebound over the coming two years. The head of Operations was equally committed to the proposition that the downturn was going to persist for at least three more years.

The two of them got into a fairly heated discussion about it. As I've seen with so many SMTs in that situation, it wasn't the passion about the issue that was surprising but the fact that they had never before talked about it. The head of Sales was floored to find out that Operations thought new home construction was going to stay in the doldrums. And the Operations head was equally dumbfounded that Sales expected a significant recovery. Yet these very senior executives had been making hundreds of decisions in the day-to-day running of the business, with each of them guided by fundamentally different assumptions about the company's core market.

"I'm amazed that you've never discussed this," I said, "since the SMT meets for four hours every Monday. What *do* you talk about?"

"We talk about customers, competitors, big orders, raw material costs, shipments, quality problems—we run the business," said the CEO. "But we only talk about end customers when there's a quality issue. We've never actually discussed what's likely to happen in the housing market as a team. That's not an operational discussion, and when we get together as a management team it's an operational meeting."

The team members quickly saw that they stood to benefit from developing a shared view of the world they were all operating in. And in those places where they couldn't come to agreement, they would at least know that, for example, Operations, which planned plant capacity and inventory levels, and Sales, which drove and forecast revenue, were proceeding under different assumptions.

Many SMTs that undertake an effort to develop a shared view often begin by looking internally at their core competencies. Others may begin by looking externally at markets and competitors, trying to build an impartial perspective on where they stand in the competitive marketplace. But neither internal capabilities nor competitors' actions are the ultimate arbiters of a company's fate. The world is. Economic, demographic, social, technological, and other powerful trends occurring in the world will ultimately determine the shape of your industry and the future of your business. If vision is about opportunities, those are the forces that should drive your early discussions. And those forces don't originate either from within your company or from within your competitors.

The external forces being discussed here dwarf any single corporation. Back in 1995, Bill Gates famously warned his colleagues at Microsoft—a seemingly invulnerable company with a lock on the future—that the firm must accommodate the coming

Internet "tidal wave" in all that it did. It's an apt comparison. The forces in the world are like enormous waves. They can engulf and overturn your industry and your company, or you can build the right surfboard to ride the wave—gaining more momentum from external forces than you could ever achieve on your own. It is at those oncoming waves that you should look first, not at your surfboard bobbing in the water.

Start with this simple question: "What can we collectively agree is happening out there?" Eventually, the discussion will move on to implications and options, but you and your team members must first agree on the facts. As John Adams said, "Facts are stubborn things, and whatever may be our wishes, our inclinations, or the dictates of our passions, they cannot alter the state of facts and evidence."

Team members at this stage are simply trying to agree on what the facts are—about the world, not the company. It's too early to discuss the company versus competitors or potential new entrants. The external forces are affecting entire industries. The relative impact on companies will vary, to be sure, but the initial discussion should focus on the forces themselves.

The process begins with the collection of data—economic, technological, social, demographic, and the like. My firm often helps clients to create a *trends book* to circulate to the team members well in advance of their first conversation so that everyone is literally on the same page. The number of trends can be large. A trends book my firm helped to compile for a computer manufacturer contained 140 pages of demographic, economic, and technological trends—everything from patterns among computer purchasers in terms of age to trends in personal savings rates to rates of wireless penetration and consumer uptake of various new digital technologies.

Knowledge of external trends may of course already be available. Many SMT members will feel they already have a handle on external events. But pulling the facts together and distributing them in a structured way helps to validate what "everyone knows" and makes sure that the conversation begins on level, fact-based, solid ground.

Clustering Trends into Drivers of Change

Addressing over 100 pages of trends and all their implications and possible combinations is of course impossible. A group can't focus on that many topics and drive to any tangible outcome. But it can distill all the trends, all the external factors, into a short (eight- to twelve-item) list of drivers of change—the big waves out there that are creating change, or will be creating change, in the industry. This is where the real conversation begins. The team goes to the 30,000-foot level and looks out to see how all those individual trends—the various ripples on the water—are forming into waves and coming toward the shore. Through a workshop process the group can synthesize these trends into the short list of forces that will drive change in the industry.

Since John Nesbitt's *Megatrends* in 1988, big-picture trend spotting has become a popular pastime. "Here," pundits declare, "are the ten forces reshaping the world." But the usefulness of such books is severely limited—any trends large enough to affect the entire public are necessarily too generic to have much meaning for a specific industry. Instead, the SMT members need to be able to talk about the ten or so forces that will be reshaping their world if they are to identify the potential threats and opportunities those forces might represent to their company.

For example, my firm's work for a European global beverage and spirits company started with the gathering of hundreds of pages of research data, market reports, industry studies, consumer forecasts—the kind of data and expert opinion that is familiar to Strategy and Marketing departments. We compiled a 150-page trends book, so that all of the senior executives would have a common reference for understanding the world in which their industry operated. The SMT members spent a day synthesizing this fact book into ten drivers of change—their common view of the fundamental forces at work that could potentially reshape their world. Here's their list:

1. Emerging markets will be a major provider of future growth, but of unknown quality/risk/timing.

2. Increased industry competitiveness will lead to a wave of M&A in our industry.

3. Developing and marketing new brands will mean establishing more direct contact with consumers instead of listening primarily to distribution partners.

4. The industry will have less control of its downstream distribution, thereby reducing margins.

5. Launching new brands will require skill sets that more closely resemble those found in luxury goods rather than in consumer packaged goods.

6. Unfavorable social trends will worsen—including increasing restrictions on alcohol consumption.

7. Regionalization and globalization will erode the country-by-country basis on which beverage companies have traditionally competed.

8. Growing, affluent, younger populations in developing markets will create new category and brand opportunities.

9. New product introductions will be increasingly difficult and expensive.

10. Consumption environments for alcoholic beverages will shift from public to private spaces.

No generic megatrends book could generate a list so tailored to a specific industry. These trends are there for all to see—just as Bill Gates and the late Steve Jobs could both see the Internet crashing down on the personal computer industry. The responses may be company specific, but drivers of change are external to any specific competitor. There are some generic items on the list— the emerging markets item (driver 1) appears on a lot of lists these days. But others are highly industry specific, like driver 10, about changing consumption environments.

The following are just a few of the trends that the team synthesized to arrive at driver 10:

- The emergence of affordable, large-screen home entertainment systems is moving group viewing of sporting events from sports bars and pubs into private homes.

- Increased telecommuting and longer working hours for men and women are decreasing the number of people stopping off in bars and pubs for a drink after work.

- Smoking bans in bars and restaurants are driving the adults who do smoke (22 percent in the United States) to socialize (and drink) in private homes.

It's far easier to have SMT-level conversations about these ten drivers of change than it would be to discuss the 150 pages in the fact book or the thousands of pages of research reports that fed into that book. Imagine your SMT with a list like this, customized to your industry, engaging in discussions about the opportunities and challenges represented by these drivers—drawing on the collective experience and knowledge of the world that is uniquely concentrated in the SMT. Unencumbered by the inward-looking approach that typically begins with the company's capabilities or by the traditional external approach that begins with competitor analysis, this conversation could well be unlike any that your team has ever had.

In the conversation about drivers of change, SMT members are certainly being asked to adopt a generalist perspective, but as generalists about the world. They're on politically neutral ground—clearly out of one another's silos and hovering up at a high enough altitude to look out at the waves in front of them. There are of course implications for all the functions represented around the table, but that conversation should come later.

Even when drivers of change for a particular industry seem obvious, self-assessments by executive teams typically show weak awareness of those drivers by managers and little or no incorporation into company plans of responses to many of the drivers. For example, after the beverage executives built their drivers of change list, I asked them to characterize, on a scale of 1 to 10, the degree to which they thought the company's top 100 managers were aware of each driver. I also had them assess the degree to which each driver was reflected in the formal plans of the company, asking them the following question for each driver: "If you were to pile up all the written documentation—the marketing plans, the capital plan, the strategic plan, and so forth—and I were to read through every page of every document, how much would I see this driver come through?"

The results for the first driver—"emerging markets will be a major provider of future growth, but of unknown quality/risk/timing"—were predictable, given that emerging market growth strategies were among the themes of the company's planning process that year. The team gave the company, on average, a score of 7.1 for management awareness of this driver and 7.8 for including this driver in its plans.

By contrast, the scores on driver 8 (about new, demographically driven category and brand opportunities) were eye-opening. This driver was underpinned by a cluster of widely available and generally understood trends. Yet awareness was rated at 5.4 and inclusion in plans at 1.9. New markets were bursting with a huge generation of potential new consumers. This major wave of change was about to wash over the industry, and yet many managers were likely to be unaware of it and the company was doing little to respond.

That doesn't mean that every driver needs to be fully embedded in company strategy—no company can build a surfboard to ride every wave. Some drivers will create momentum for one company whereas competitors will choose to follow other sets of trends. But choosing not to leverage change differs dramatically from being unaware that it is occurring.

For the beverage company this single list of ten drivers of change provoked a set of extremely productive conversations and actions. For example, to respond to demographically driven opportunities, the company launched a set of initiatives around understanding and leveraging changes in the young adult market segment. Within a year it had acquired and launched brands aimed squarely at that rapidly growing segment, revamped aspects of distribution to get access to a larger share of the market, and made some critical hires in the marketing and product development functions to stay more in tune with this user category over time. Marketing, Product Development, HR, Distribution, Finance, and Business Development all had a role in repositioning the company to catch the wave it might otherwise have missed, and this coordinated organizational response began at the SMT offsite.

That's why the SMT—not the Strategic Planning Department or Marketing function—should drive this look outside the four walls of the company. Although individual groups may have a role in the prework to make the conversation happen, the conversation needs to occur among the SMT members themselves. Their conversations about drivers of change are the starting point for alignment of the entire organization around a shared set of assumptions about reality. This process contrasts starkly with the more typical practice of adopting a generic goal—such as "to be number one or number two in all our markets"—and calling it a vision.

After the SMT has considered trends, clustered them into drivers of change, and discussed their implications for the industry and the company, the CEO can be confident that the leaders of key parts of the business, and the hundreds of decisions they are making each month, are at last being driven by a shared view of the world. And because the members of the SMT collectively represent all parts of the business, that group is both a unique and an ideal medium for communicating the message across the entire organization.

The alignment of the SMT around a shared view of the outside world also pays off when the team turns to another of the critical conversations it should have—the development of a competitor view. This is a much more familiar conversation for many SMTs, and it is usually done in the form of a SWOT analysis, an examination of **S**trengths, **W**eaknesses, **O**pportunities, and **T**hreats. The goal is to understand who the competitors are, their strengths and weaknesses, and what they are likely to do. But that conversation, too, will be greatly enriched because it rests on the foundation of the SMT members' shared view of the industry's major drivers of change.

For example, their shared understanding of a driver could well lead the team to see a potential competitor that they might otherwise have overlooked. (Think of the fast-disappearing newspapers, flattened by blogs, Craigslist, and Monster.com—not other news outlets.) Similarly, the team's understanding of industry change could also make sense of competitor moves that might otherwise be opaque, or it could help the team to identify white space in which competitors are not playing. A number of methods—like scenario planning and war-gaming—are available to help teams explore competitive and market dynamics. A well-developed list of drivers of change can power those discussions as well. Conversely, a lack of team alignment around external forces means that time spent on competitors and markets may fall short on long-term impact.

Bill Gates, having foreseen the Internet tidal wave, declared that Microsoft would embrace what is now termed *cloud computing*—applications and information stored and accessed both centrally and remotely by personal computers. Steve Jobs, having seen the same wave, declared that we were entering a world of "post-PC" devices. Apple then launched three blockbuster devices—the iPod, the iPhone, and the iPad. In 1995, the year of Gates's Internet memo, Microsoft's market capitalization was ten times greater than Apple's. Today, Apple is 50 percent more valuable than Microsoft. Bill Gates and his team confronted the tidal wave. Steve Jobs and his team embraced it and built a surfboard to ride it to success, by reinventing the music business, the cellular phone, and the publishing industry and, most recently, by reinventing the personal computer itself.

Understanding Capabilities and Assets

If drivers of change are the waves heading toward whole industries, your organization's capabilities and assets are the surfboards it can use to ride those waves. It's better situated to ride some waves than others—and so are its competitors. You and your SMT need to understand what the organization has that enables it to ride a wave and win, and what components its surfboard is missing that the organization will need to build.

The beverage company saw a wave of younger drinkers emerging in certain markets. The company's capabilities and assets for riding that wave included an extensive and effective distribution system and deep expertise in media buying and product development. One of the capabilities its SMT identified as lacking was expertise in marketing packaged goods to the twenty-one- to thirty-five-year-old age cohort. So the company hired an executive from a packaged goods company with the requisite expertise and engaged an ad agency team that was adept at reaching this younger demographic. The result was the successful development and launch of several new youth-oriented beverages, and significant revenue growth.

The SMT's capabilities and assets conversation begins with a consideration of what makes the company distinctive. In other words, what makes us *us*? The reflexive answer is of course "our people." But there are simple mechanisms for pushing the conversation past such clichés. I often do it by asking the SMT some simple questions: If your competitors could wave a magic wand and take two things from you—any asset, any capability, any aspect of your company—what would they take? If you could take two things from them, what would you choose?

I can think of many things that a consulting firm might want to take from competitors: McKinsey's well-deserved credibility in the boardroom and C-suite; BCG's creativity and collective intellect applied against tough business problems; Accenture's reach, scale, and bulletproof reputation in the technology sphere. These are some of the capabilities and assets that make these firms distinctive. A big-box retailer might envy Wal-Mart's capability in supplier management or its skill in logistics. Companies that offer high-tech products would love to wave that magic wand and appropriate Apple's excellence in design or its almost cultlike following among consumers. A luxury goods company might envy Tiffany's strong association with a specific shade of blue, or Ralph Lauren's unique ability to tap into deep cultural archetypes and turn them into timeless designs.

Some of the capabilities and assets that a company possesses might not be obvious, emerging only in the course of the conversation. Executives tend to define their companies by what they sell or by the customers who buy from them. The obvious answers may seem too obvious, and the subtle answers can often come across as too theoretical or as *consultantese*. But by collectively pursuing the answers to the questions of what it is that the company truly does better or knows more about than anyone else out there, the SMT members can sow the seeds of sustainable growth.

Walking the Boundaries of the Company: Testing Walls and Fences

In the process of aligning around a common view of the world and the company, one of the most productive conversations SMT members can have is also one of the rarest. So rare, in fact, that it doesn't have a commonly used name, as competitor analysis or scenario planning do, for example. I call it *walking the walls and fences*, and it consists of collectively testing and affirming the boundaries of a company's business model. Walls are the boundaries around any business that are assumed to be immovable—*the things we do not do*—so much so that executive teams don't even bother to approach them. But by challenging these assumptions, teams can discover that walls are sometimes fences—boundaries that can in fact be moved if there's a compelling reason to do so, opening up strategic space for the company.

As with their understandings of the external world, different executives often turn out to have strikingly different understandings of what the boundaries of their business really are. For example, when I ran strategy for Sears in the 1990s we were kicking around the idea of acquiring Home Depot. Ed Liddy, then the Sears CFO, and later the CEO of both Allstate and AIG, thought it would be a great fit. The company's Craftsman tools and Kenmore appliances would have great synergy with Home Depot's product assortment, and we had retail management expertise and a broad and loyal customer base.

Ed Brennan, then the Sears CEO, didn't like the idea. Home Depot distributed perishable items like live plants and items like lumber that also need to be fresh when sold. Other than soft goods, Sears didn't sell anything that couldn't sit in a warehouse without losing value, and even the soft goods tended to be items that wouldn't go out of fashion rapidly. Perishable goods were just not our kind of business, he said, and at that moment a boundary was defined. Until this discussion the two Eds had held very different views without knowing it, but once the boundary had emerged they could then address the question of whether it was an immovable wall or an easily moved fence.

For achieving breakthroughs through new opportunities or finding new possibilities in adjacent spaces, there is no better method than testing walls and fences. And in cases where a company is looking not just for new opportunities but also for a redesign of its business model, understanding the business's current boundaries—their precise contours and degree of rigidity—is an indispensable first step.

You can prepare for the walls and fences conversation by soliciting from the top executive team and from representatives of the company's various geographies and markets a list of the rules of the business believed to be inviolable. You will get plenty of these perceived rules—boundaries tend to be well known and broadly assumed. The list can then be winnowed down to the ten to twenty critical boundaries that govern management behavior. The SMT can then work through which of these barriers are legitimate and which are not, which are really immoveable walls and which are moveable fences—only later turning to a conversation about the growth opportunities that might be opened up by relocating a particular boundary.

For example, a large financial services company regarded this rule as one of its inviolable boundaries: "We will not make an acquisition that will add substantially to headcount." When the list of walls and fences was discussed, the CEO reacted sharply: "That's wrong. Five or six years ago when we were cost cutting we rejected some acquisition candidates because they brought high headcounts, but that's ancient history. If a potential acquisition is accretive we'd certainly look at it, regardless of how many employees they might have." When the CFO replied that headcount was in fact still an active screening criterion for acquisition candidates, it became clear that the organization was fully respecting a wall that in the CEO's eyes should have been removed years ago. How many potential acquisitions never got to be considered by the SMT as a result?

There's an interesting postscript to this story. The day after the walls and fences discussion had identified headcount as a widely understood but unintended limitation on the company's business model, the SMT was engaged in a discussion about a potential new venture. "If we were to do that," the chief counsel said, "I'd need a few new attorneys on my staff." The head of Product chimed in, "I'd have to add two or three people to work on that full-time." Pretty soon, the SMT members had identified ten to fifteen new positions that would be required to pursue what could have been a major new growth opportunity. "Well," added the CEO, "we need to look very carefully at this one. We're talking about potentially adding a lot of people here."

Although the company isn't particularly employee intensive, given its revenues and profit, it did have several thousand people. The fact that this enormous potential opportunity might, initially, involve hiring a handful of people appeared to be costing the idea a tremendous amount of momentum. Finally, a member of the SMT piped up: "Wait a minute. Yesterday we said that headcount wasn't a wall when it came to new business opportunities if the economics made sense. Now we're talking about holding back on one of the best new business ideas we've heard in years because it would mean adding a dozen or so senior staff. Which is it? Is headcount a wall or isn't it? No wonder our people are confused."

The SMT of a major industrial company identified more than fifteen widely held assumptions about what the company would *never* do. Here are a few of those presumed walls:

- We do not enter businesses that would lower average gross margins.
- We use our brand only on our core products.
- We will not go into businesses even marginally competitive with our customers.
- We do not allow others to use our manufacturing facilities.

Some of the fifteen walls were validated. Some of the walls had simply been built up from company folklore. Some were based on inferences drawn from the past behavior of top executives, and others were derived from written policies. But the important thing is that even though there was consensus among the SMT members that some of the walls were in fact walls that couldn't be moved, in most cases there wasn't much agreement about whether an individual item was a wall, a fence, or a phantom belief with no basis in current reality.

The prohibition against entering businesses that lowered average margins was news to the CEO. "Our margins are so strong that almost any new business we are likely to enter will lower the average," he said incredulously. "But if it's a good business that will increase shareholder value, of course we would consider the deal. We'll never grow if we consider maintaining current margins a criterion for acquisitions. When did we ever say we wanted that?"

The widespread belief on the part of managers or members of the SMT that such rules are inviolable has an unfortunate effect: many innovative business ideas simply never get considered. Why propose an idea that everybody knows will never fly? Why beat your head against a wall?

At a global provider of investment services, one of the walls was believed to be a strict prohibition against going into banking. Customers had expressed a desire for banking products, and these could provide a major new avenue of growth for the company. But everyone knew that the CEO had always rejected moves into banking services.

Instead of shying away from discussing it, the team walked up to the barrier and tested it. The executives asked why the barrier was there, what purpose it served, and what the real nature of the constraint might be. Under this kind of explicit questioning, it emerged that the real desire was to avoid anything that would bring the company under supervision from additional regulatory agencies. Once the true boundary of the wall was carefully defined, the company was free to offer any types of products that were within the purview of the company's existing regulators. The immovable wall standing between the company and banking services turned out, once challenged, to be a relatively moveable fence. There was significant new competitive space to enter between the location of the former, well-understood wall and the newly defined business limit. That's where real growth lies—on the other side of the things you think you don't do.

It's important to distinguish between testing and moving walls and fences and just relabeling what a company does. My late father came home from his long-time barber one day and announced, "Phil Rosa isn't a barber anymore." "Did he go out of business?" I asked. "No," my dad replied, "he went to a special school for a few days and now he's a hairstylist." "What's the difference?" I asked. "Five bucks," Dad replied.

Like my father's barber, a lot of management teams spent time not too long ago reconceiving what business their companies were really in. Inspired by the work of Gary Hamel and C. K. Prahalad on core competencies, executives drilled down to their company's core competency and then restated that competency in broad general terms meant to expand the horizons of the business. A well-known copier manufacturer redefined its business as "document management." That one made sense. But it seemed also that every regional bus company became an "intermodal, intercity, human transport enterprise." Unless you genuinely test boundaries—the things you don't do—and specifically identify whether they might be moved and how far, such exercises may simply put old wine in new bottles.

One of the most important jobs the SMT can do is to identify specific boundaries and understand the potential value of relocating them. The team should also clearly communicate those rules that should tightly constrain management behavior and those that should be considered moveable or be removed completely. Otherwise, as with conflicting views of the world, decisions may be reached at lower management levels on the basis of assumptions that are incorrect, outmoded, or misinterpretations. Of course, some walls are perfectly justifiable, even desirable, boundaries around the business. Not all walls are fences. But leaders whose teams know the difference often achieve surprising results.

Defining and Selecting Opportunities

An SMT whose members have come to a mutual understanding of drivers of change, competitors, internal capabilities and assets, and walls and fences is prepared to develop a set of growth opportunities. For example, it was clear to many that the economics of book publishing and distribution would create an opportunity for the e-book to emerge, just as the iPod had helped to trigger the electronic distribution of music. The drivers of change were clear—bits had replaced atoms and content had become detached from physical form. Portable electronic devices were becoming cheaper. Batteries were lasting longer. Screen resolution was improving rapidly. Bandwidth for over-the-air distribution was becoming cheaper. But there was a chicken-and-egg problem—people wouldn't embrace the e-book until a viable reader came along, and a reader required a base of available content.

Amazon.com took a look at these changes happening in its world and then at its unique capabilities and assets: relationships with the world's leading publishers and with readers, an ability to sell both content and devices, and server capacity to handle the distribution. But one thing was missing: Amazon did not have a viable e-book reader to sell. And one of the presumed walls at Amazon was that Amazon.com didn't manufacture things. The company was a store, not a manufacturer.

But as Amazon.com founder Jeff Bezos told *BusinessWeek*:

> When [companies] think about extending their business into some new area, the first question is "why should we do that—we don't have any skills in that area." That approach puts a finite lifetime on a company, because the world changes, and what used to be cutting-edge skills have turned into something your customers may not need anymore. A much more stable strategy is to start with "what do my customers need?" Then do an inventory of the gaps in your skills. Kindle is a great example. If we set our strategy by what our skills happen to be rather than by what our customers need, we never would have done it. We had to go out and hire people who know how to build hardware devices and create a whole new competency for the company.[1]

At some point, the leadership at Amazon must have had some searching discussions that were, in effect, about walls and fences. The presumed wall—*we do not manufacture hardware*—turned out to be a moveable fence. And moving that boundary enabled not one opportunity but several: manufacturing and distributing the Kindle; distributing e-books for publishers; distributing self-published e-books; and distributing magazines, blogs, and newspapers on a subscription model.

The result? Amazon has 70 to 80 percent of the e-book market and has built a $5 billion business, with almost a million titles available.

Discovering drivers of change, identifying capabilities and assets (those you have and those you need), and redefining business boundaries aren't the only stages in building strategies or identifying opportunities. But these are the critical conversations that a Senior Management Team needs to engage in, because organizational alignment around the issues is a prerequisite to putting a successful vision into place.

Ultimately, these conversations prepare the organization to design specific strategic initiatives, with action plans, accountabilities, and business cases. But there are likely to be scores of other initiatives already under way, with all parts of the organization pushing their projects and clamoring for additional resources. Rationalizing and integrating these initiatives can be one of the most difficult and frustrating tasks that any organization faces. But as the next chapter details, the job can be made much easier and more productive when the CEO and the SMT know how to leverage the team's unique advantages of seniority, representativeness, and status through another set of conversations that can't occur anywhere else.

Note

1. "Bezos on Innovation," *BusinessWeek* (April 17, 2008).

CHAPTER 9

Prioritize and Integrate Initiatives to Hit the Strategic Bull's-Eye

Even the best-run companies are likely to have scores of initiatives under way, with each part of the organization supporting projects it believes to be worthy, and everyone competing for the same pool of resources. A few projects—typically a dozen or less—may be intended to fulfill the handful of overarching, direction-setting strategy objectives that emerge from an SMT-level strategic discussion. But in addition there are the myriad smaller programs, task forces, or other activities that go above and beyond the day-to-day responsibilities of a single function.

Initiatives constitute a significant part of an organization's activities: a plant expansion, a new training program, a move into a new market, an IT upgrade, and many other efforts, large and small, single function and cross-functional. Perhaps because they are widely dispersed through the company and often occurring several levels down in the organization, they can easily remain invisible to CEOs unless there is an explicit effort to unearth them.

So why bother looking into initiatives at all? Why not just leave them alone and maintain the status quo, layering major new strategic initiatives on top of the current set as required? Because CEOs then find that corporate resources are being sucked into a multitude of activities of widely varying quality and relevance while resources are unavailable for vital activities.

"It reminds me of the old-fashioned plate spinner at the circus," says Bob Selander, the retired president and CEO of MasterCard. "He has five, six, seven, eight plates at the end of sticks and keeps them all going. Is he going to go for nine, or is he going to go back and give a tap to that first one to keep it going? There's a limit. You can only get so many plates going before you start hearing the crash of china on the floor."

When it comes to people—one of the most important resources of all—it's always the same group of players who are being drawn in multiple directions, each of them with a day job to attend to as well. "There is a limit to how much an individual can take on at any given point in time," says Selander. "And if you put more on their backs than they can carry, then sooner or later they're going to buckle."

Two of the most difficult and frustrating challenges that any organization faces are prioritizing initiatives and then integrating them in a way that best achieves the company's strategic objectives. This high-level management of initiatives—both prioritization and integration—is the bridge between setting a strategy and seeing it successfully implemented. If the CEO and Senior Management Team (SMT) can get the organization focused on a limited set of critical initiatives; develop clarity around objectives, resources, milestones, and measures of success for each; and collectively track and manage them, then they have a fighting chance of reaching their strategic goals. Otherwise, strategies tend to get stuck in the mud.

This task can be almost impossible if not approached thoughtfully. Many CEOs rightly see that the SMT, with its unique advantages of experience, representativeness, and status, is the ideal venue for the critically important prioritization and integration conversations. But they often fail to structure these conversations in a way that leverages the unique characteristics of the team while also overcoming its inherent limitations and the inherent difficulty of the job.

Asking the Nearly Impossible: Prioritizing Initiatives

Consider the initial approach to prioritization taken by the CEO of a consumer packaged goods company. My firm had just conducted an inventory of his company's initiatives—a list of all the significant projects planned or under way throughout the organization that project sponsors had identified as being "over and above our conducting business as usual." The number of initiatives we had identified in a few days of effort? One hundred and ten. The CEO was livid. "This is ridiculous," he said. "No wonder I can't find anyone to do the things I want done. They're all racing around chasing different things. It's chaos. We've got to shut some of these down."

In the many inventories of initiatives we have undertaken over the years, I've found time and again that the number we identify is often double or triple what the CEO expects. We rarely find fewer than 50 to 60. Usually it's 80 to 120, and we've sometimes identified over 150 active initiatives under way in a client company. Even in organizations that think they run a tight ship, there are likely to be scores of initiatives planned or in progress at any given time. Before undertaking an inventory I will often say to the CEO, "I bet you a dollar we'll find at least 75." Because most initiatives are invisible to CEOs, they're skeptical. "No way," they'll say. "Maybe 20 or 30." And then the list of 90 or 100 or 125 lands on their desks.

Most CEOs react as the CEO of the consumer packaged goods company did: "I'm going to call a meeting of my team, take out my red pen, and we're going to start drawing lines through most of these."

"It won't work," I told him as diplomatically as I could.

It never does. Each of those initiatives has an owner somewhere in the organization who really believes in it. These aren't stupid people, and they're not wasteful people. They're undertaking these initiatives because they believe they're the right thing to do. Asking them to shut down an initiative is like asking a kid to give away one of his puppies. And in some cases you'll be asking them to do something even harder—to give away the puppy of one of their subordinates and then justify it to that person the next day. Besides, how will your SMT decide? Most of them don't know a thing about most of these initiatives—they're taking place outside of their functional areas, or below the level of their visibility. They won't have any idea how to evaluate the relative merits of each other's initiatives, much less be able to rank them.

"They'll have to choose," he said. "It's what they get paid for."

He was right to be impatient. The many initiatives on any business's list are likely to vary greatly in quality and in importance to the company. Further, pursuing all the initiatives simultaneously would require virtually limitless resources. Such a proliferation of projects suggests a company that is unfocused, undisciplined, and unable to allocate resources effectively. Why not rectify the situation with a few strokes of a pen?

But when I next spoke with the CEO his anger had turned to deep frustration. He had convened his SMT and the executives had struggled mightily to rationalize the list of initiatives. They had managed to cut projects that were already on life support, were extremely trivial, or had only tepid backing. They had also resorted to gaming the system, shortening the list by merging two or three initiatives into one header without actually changing anything. But they still had an unrealistically long list of projects, almost all of which seemed like good ideas, at least to someone.

That's when the frustration set in. Anyone can eliminate manifestly bad or virtually dead initiatives. It's usually done simply by considering each initiative in turn and burrowing down into it to see if it's inherently worthwhile. Those that are obviously weak or irrelevant can easily be tossed out. Those that are clearly worthwhile cannot. Invariably, the result is a long list of inherently good ideas. When initiatives are considered one by one, it's the rare initiative that can be immediately dismissed.

Compounding the difficulty, each of these good ideas has a backer, either in the room or further down in the organization. Initiative owners can be extremely passionate. When I was a division president at Dial Corporation we had a bright and ambitious group product manager I'll call Frank Sanders. At that time, Dial was in personal care products, like Dial soap, as well as food products, like Armour Star canned meat. Frank wanted to initiate a line of frozen soups—he already had the lab hard at work on it. He believed that there was a market opening for a high-quality, microwavable frozen soup, and that Dial could create one that would generate significant profits. Frank was the model of what was known at the time as an *intrapreneur*—someone with a strong entrepreneurial streak and adept at getting things accomplished inside a sometimes bureaucratic environment.

Three months into the project, Frank and his boss were walking back from a budget review where the frozen soup initiative had been slammed by the head of Operations. It was clear that Dial wasn't going into the soup business or the frozen food business, each of which has unique manufacturing and logistics requirements that were simply beyond the willingness of Operations to support. Because the president had been at the meeting and had supported Operations in the decision, there was little chance for reconsideration. The initiative was dead, and Frank's boss told him to shut it down immediately and move on.

From the point of view of the president, the head of Operations, and Frank's boss that was that. A red line had been drawn through the frozen soup initiative, and the resources would be quickly redeployed to more productive uses.

What they hadn't taken into account was Frank.

Six months later I ran into him in the new products lab, and he invited me to a *cutting*—the tasting of a new food product under development. This new product was a soup, frozen minestrone. "Frank," I said, "we're not going into the frozen soups business. I was at the budget review. I saw the wooden stake driven through its heart."

"I know," he said. "This isn't the frozen soup initiative. That's been dead for a while. This is part of the new ethnic foods line I'm going to develop."

Frank had slipped his frozen soup project out of his left pocket and into his right. His explanation was laughable, but his passion wasn't. And it's that passion you're up against when you try to kill someone else's initiative.

Consider the experience of a global financial services company. The CEO asked the line managers on his team—the head of North America, the head of International, and the head of Product—to determine the five most important initiatives in each of their areas. That wasn't a bad start—it's certainly a good idea to ask each of your key subordinates to rank order their individual priorities for the coming year. But then he asked the three of them to collectively prioritize all fifteen initiatives, agree on the top ten, and rank order them.

He might as well have locked them in a steel cage with machetes. They might have agreed on a number one priority, but with only a limited set of major initiatives destined to survive with full funding, there was no way an executive with responsibility for a huge piece of the business was going to concede, for example, that his number two priority might be less important than someone else's number three or to agree to any other ordering that might leave his critical projects on the cutting-room floor.

The Real Source of the Difficulty

The problem isn't that senior teams don't know what's important or that CEOs are unreasonable. People who have risen to the top of an organization are typically seasoned and intelligent. In addition, compensation plans at the top of most organizations are typically structured to encourage managers to look out for the overall best interests of the company. Yet rationalizing initiatives, or even prioritizing them, remains enormously difficult.

At this point, you may feel tempted to reply, "Oh, come on, any halfway decent senior executive could make these decisions by simply applying a little common sense."

Maybe they could, within their own domains. But it's likely that each member of the team, representing his or her specific area, has his or her own version of common sense. What looks self-evident to the head of Marketing may mean little to the head of a midsize division, and vice versa. As the eminent anthropologist Clifford Geertz observed, common sense is often defined as "what anyone with his head screwed on straight cannot help but think." But as he found, different cultures have far different views of what those commonsensical things are. The same goes for the different functional and divisional cultures in most large organizations. What is needed is not individual common sense, but a *common* common sense among all the participants in the prioritization conversation—an alignment around a common point of view about what makes sense.

But the way this conversation is usually handled—by having the team rank order all the initiatives—is almost guaranteed to keep that alignment from emerging. Why? Because it runs head-on into all four of the fundamental conflicts, discussed in Chapter Four, that lie at the heart of senior management teams:

- First, team members are being asked to behave as Knights of the Round Table, taking the CEO's perspective. Certainly, rationalizing initiatives does require team members to assume a generalist stance. But asking them to rank order initiatives and justify their rankings puts them in the untenable position of either lobbing grenades into another team member's territory or defending their own area's initiatives from challenge. At the extremes, the result is either silence or turf war, neither of which will produce a common view. The most probable scenario is some combination of the two extremes, with some members contributing nothing and the more aggressive members dominating.

- Second, this approach overlooks the partly legislative nature of the group. Every one of the initiatives being considered for the chopping block is owned either by someone in the room or by someone who works for someone in the room. Team members are being asked to return to their constituents and say, "I just left a meeting where they cut your initiative," or, "I agreed to cancel that project that we've all been gearing up for." Imagine the reaction that a Senator from Iowa would get when he told the folks back home that he had agreed to cut ethanol subsidies, or that a congresswoman from Newport News, Virginia, would get after confessing to having helped pull the plug on a planned aircraft carrier. Backing away from a long-held position might take weeks or months of prework on a leader's part and rarely occurs on a spur-of-the-moment basis.

- Third, the more powerful members of the team—the Californias and New Yorks—may be able to protect certain initiatives regardless of their real merit, and the resulting ranking of the initiatives could reflect merely the rank of their sponsors. I remember one powerful division president telling her peers on the SMT, "At the end of the day I should have the most say about what initiatives get funded because, after all, I'm paying for them." A week after the meeting, one of her functional colleagues was still steaming over her comment. "Where does she get off saying that she's paying for them?" he complained. "She may pay her mortgage. She may pay her car payments. She may pay her kids' tuition. But this is the company's money, not hers. Why should she have all the votes about where the company spends its money?"

When I discussed the issue with the division president she had an equally strong point of view. "I've got a P&L. He doesn't. It's that simple. Every dollar he spends impacts my division's results, since I carry the lion's share of the allocations for corporate expenditures. You bet I've got the votes—otherwise what constraints would there be on functional allocations going through the roof?"

- Fourth, as explained in the discussion of Condorcet's voting paradox in Chapter Four, the inherent difficulties arising when three or more people try to rank three or more preferences mean that the team is being asked to do something that at times literally cannot be done. Even the existence of clear individual preferences for the ranking of the initiatives may not enable the group to develop a ranking, owing to the circular rather than linear logic resulting from the multiple choices made.

If rationalizing initiatives is so difficult for an SMT, why not just bypass this particular group altogether? Because all of the alternatives are worse. If you ask a kitchen cabinet to rationalize initiatives, you will not only leave many parts of the organization feeling unrepresented but you are also likely to exacerbate whatever feelings of disempowerment members of the top team already harbor. If the CEO takes it upon herself to do the prioritizing, in splendid isolation, she's asking for a world of trouble—a relentless stream of one-on-one meetings with members of her team as they lobby to keep their favored initiatives. Without detailed knowledge of each initiative, she's setting herself up to do as much potential harm as good.

Appointing an ad hoc initiatives rationalization team is another possibility, as long as each function and area and initiative is represented, but the organization already has a team that's representative of functions and areas—the SMT itself. Besides, if each initiative were also represented on this special initiatives team, the representatives might see it as their duty to defend their turf even more strongly than the SMT members would.

Perhaps one of the worst alternatives is to outsource the job to consultants. This is certainly one of the most frequently used options—initiative rationalization is a big cash cow for many consulting firms. Its appeal is twofold. The consultants can do a detailed analysis of the initiatives and put in place a weighted scoring system to rank them. But the primary appeal, I suspect, is that blame for cutting favored initiatives can be laid at the feet of the consultants. Overall, this approach is nothing less than an abdication of the top team's responsibility for managing the company.

As the CEO of the packaged goods company rightly understood, the top team is the body best suited for the job. Just as with the vision conversation, the SMT represents all parts of the organization; the members are highly experienced, and they operate at a level that enables them to appreciate the corporate perspective of maximizing the value of the whole. The solution is not to bypass what is far and away the best team for the job but instead to stop asking it to do the impossible. Instead, structure these critical conversations in a way that leads to results without absolute rankings and that produces alignment instead of acrimony.

Changing the Conversation

A number of systems have been devised to try to force the rank ordering of initiatives. Some organizations use initiative weighting and scoring systems that come out of the world of project management. Criteria are established and weighted and each initiative is assigned points for how well it fulfills each criterion. Then each initiative's points are multiplied by the weight of the criteria it helps fulfill. So, for example, an initiative that scored moderately well on a heavily weighted criterion would outrank an initiative that scored very well on a more lightly weighted criterion. In any case, the calculations render a mathematically determined rank order for each of the initiatives.

Colleges are ranked in much the same way. The ranking system assigns a weight to factors such as student/teacher ratio, alumni giving, number of distinguished faculty, and so on. The individual schools are then assigned points for how well they perform against each criterion. The points are multiplied by the weight of each criterion, added up, and the school lands precisely at a specific ranking in the pecking order of colleges and universities.

Organizations that use weighted systems to rationalize initiatives do get several things right:

- It's always a good idea to begin by clearly stating the criteria, asking what the organization is trying to optimize.

- The goal is to evaluate the merits of initiatives relative to each other, not in isolation.

- By leaving aside the question of which initiatives will be funded, the process is made easier; the initial goal is to assess only the initiatives' relative importance. In other words, you can set the priorities and then draw the over/under line later, when it's clearer what resources are available and how many initiatives can be funded.

But companies (and those who rank colleges) get it wrong in several important ways. The apparent precision of the rankings is largely an illusion created by the mechanistic scoring system. How can you precisely compare Vassar to Caltech? MIT to Swarthmore? Is that SAP upgrade exactly two points superior to outsourcing routine legal work? Is Harvard really slightly better than Yale, and are both precisely a point or two better than Princeton?

Corporate initiatives are too important to be left to such mechanistic assessment and spurious accuracy. At the level of the SMT, there should be a rich discussion, not a machine for short-circuiting it. Further, it's easy to game the system—members of the team may succeed in assigning unreasonably high scores to specific attributes of initiatives they favor, given that many of the points are assigned on a subjective basis.

As we will see, there are more productive and ultimately easier ways to determine relative preference rankings than to artificially force things into quantitative systems. Far from reducing complexity, a mechanistic system in fact introduces a further set of biases, which are masked by its seemingly logical process.

Consider instead the course taken by the consumer packaged goods (CPG) company. After the CEO's failed attempt to do a one-meeting, red-pencil cancelling of initiatives—the almost universal response of leaders when they first find projects sprouting like weeds in every corner of the company—he and his team embarked on a much different kind of conversation. What's important in this example is not any particular workshop design but instead that, no matter what means are used, the goal is to have a discussion-based prioritization of initiatives *relative to each other*, using techniques that neither create a false precision nor run aground on the inherent difficulties of deciding.

My firm began with the CPG company by going back to square one—the entire list of 110 initiatives. We identified an owner (or sponsor) for each initiative—which in some cases was difficult—and we had each owner fill out a one-page template for his or her project. The page asked for the name of the initiative and the name of its owner, the background issue, a listing of the people involved and their roles, a high-level cost-benefit analysis (nothing more complicated than sources of cost and sources of benefit—no quantification at this stage), the measures of outcomes, the definition of success, and the major milestones achieved or anticipated and the timing of these milestones. Each initiative owner was then asked to assess his or her initiative on a two-by-two matrix: *must do/should do* and *do immediately/defer.* (So it was possible, for example, to have an initiative that was a *must do/defer.*)

We then met with each of the SMT members and asked them to assess the portfolio of initiatives that fell under their purview and to determine an initial placement on a three-by-three matrix: *must do/should do/nice to do* and *now/soon/later.* The additional categories were added on the assumption that SMT members, with a broader view of the initiatives in their domains, would be able to apply that extra level of nuance. The question would no longer be whether an initiative had intrinsic merit but where it roughly stood in relation to the team's other initiatives.

Thus the initiative owners and SMT members were addressing both importance and urgency. Assigning initiatives to the categories of *must do*, *should do*, and *nice to do* is to evaluate them according to their importance. And those categories are sufficiently broad to be easily understood yet sufficiently clear to provide actual meaning: These are things we *must* do. These are things we *should* do, but if things get tight we can get by without doing them, at least for now. These are things that would be *nice* to do if we have sufficient resources available. All very clear and very direct.

But organizations struggle not only with what initiatives to undertake but with when to undertake them. In my experience these discussions of urgency often bog down in absurdly precise projections of timing. Groups try to wedge initiatives into very specific time windows—zero to three months, three to six months, six to twelve months, and so on—even though many initiatives will take months to put together and launch and may not pay off for quarters or even years. Yet people can feel that initiatives that aren't launched immediately may never occur, and so the question of timing can turn into a de facto effort to rank order, with all the same difficulties and the frustrations that effort causes in other situations. Breaking the issue of importance out into a separate dimension—*must do/should do/nice to do*—keeps the time axis cleaner, because it's no longer being used as a surrogate for importance. Instead, the discussion of time stays focused on the proper issue: When do we start?

As with the dimension of importance, I divide the dimension of time into thirds. In the past I had used two categories—*now* and *later*—to indicate things that should start right now and things that shouldn't. But clients saw *later* as too broad, so I introduced a third category: *soon*. When asked to define *soon* I have a standard response—it's not *now* but before *later*. Remarkable as it seems (and for reasons I'll explain in a moment), it's much easier to assign initiatives to the three time categories of *now*, *soon*, and *later* than to fit them on a timeline, and far more productive.

Armed with these six categories on two dimensions—*must do*, *should do*, and *nice to do* for importance, and *now*, *soon*, and *later* for time—an SMT can have a discussion on initiatives and priorities along the nine-cell matrix that results. This conversation can help the CEO and the SMT to rapidly achieve an enormous amount of organizational alignment.

The ninety-five completed individual initiative sheets for the CPG company were bound in a book, tabbed by functions, and circulated to members of the SMT well in advance of the meeting in which they would take them up. (Fifteen initiatives had vanished either when we asked for a sponsor to be identified or asked for the basic one-page template to be completed.) This prereading, which would be supplemented by discussion in the meeting itself, would bring each member up to speed on each initiative that was seeking meaningful resources for the coming year.

For the meeting, the SMT members' three-by-three initial placements were collated into one large wall chart displayed in the front of the room. On seeing the chart categories, the CEO asked, somewhat incredulously, "Where is *stop doing*?" I said that realistically no *stop doing* would ever make it to this level and that we weren't even going to try to identify *stop doings* in this meeting. We didn't want SMT members to go back to their constituents and inform them that any initiatives had been killed. Instead, such initiatives would be assigned to the *nice to do* category, defined as "the things we would do if we had unlimited resources." This tactic is not unlike a parent's when a child requests an ice cream sundae and the parent says, "we'll see," rather than no. This answer is in effect the same as an unambiguous no, but it is much easier to accept.

Not surprisingly, there were very few initiatives in the *nice to do* or *later* cells on the matrix at the outset. There rarely are. Initially, virtually every initiative shows up in the *must do/now* cell—far outstripping the capability of the organization to resource, let alone successfully execute, all of these initiatives.

In a similar exercise for a division of a utility company, I recall that the head of compliance not only had all her initial placements for her initiatives in the center of the *must do/now* cell but also walked up to the chart and drew a circle around them with a red marker. The head of the division asked, "What's with the red line?"

"It means these are inviolable *must do*'s," she said. "They're compliance—you *have* to do them."

The division head pulled one of her initiatives off the chart and held it up. "If we don't do this, will I or any member of this team go to jail?"

"What?" she asked.

"If we don't do the things written on this piece of paper, will we be in violation of the law and will someone go to jail?"

"Well ... no," she said.

"Okay then. It's open for discussion. That's the criterion—whether or not someone will go to jail. Nobody gets a free pass here. You have to *earn* a *must do*. Otherwise we're not going to get anywhere in this discussion."

In the case of the CPG company, the members of the team, seeing everyone's initiatives deployed on the matrix next to their own, were given the opportunity to adjust their individual placements. A few did so, but as I've seen in so many other instances, their adjustments involved moving an initiative from *must do/now* to *must do/soon*. A few fell to the *nice to do* row, but it was still fairly desolate. The overwhelming majority of the initiatives remained clustered in *must do/now*.

After the team members' adjustments, I pulled what I believed to be one of the most important and urgent initiatives from the crowded *must do/now* cell and initiated a discussion of it—first, in terms of whether it was really a matter for the team to manage or was the responsibility of another group or individual (possibly an individual in the room). For example, improving safety at a plant in Ohio might more properly be a primary responsibility for the head of Operations or Manufacturing, though the SMT might want to stay informed on the matter. Such initiatives are more a matter of day-to-day operations than strategy. For purposes of the prioritization conversation, those initiatives could be set aside.

Once it was agreed that the SMT should maintain some degree of oversight of the initiative, the discussion then turned to whether the company *had* to do it and had to do it *now*. The group readily agreed that the initiative was both important and urgent, so the Post-it on which it was written was transferred to the *must do/now* cell on a second, empty wall chart.

Once the group members agreed that they owned a second initiative, they were asked to discuss it relative to the prior initiative. This is where such discussions really take off, as the group works to answer the question, Is the second initiative roughly as important and urgent as the first one we discussed? Less so? More so? There was no discussion of the initiative's intrinsic merits. And it had been made emphatically clear at the outset that the question was not whether an initiative was going to be funded or killed.

Once rough consensus had been achieved, the second initiative was placed accordingly on the new chart—in this case, slightly below the first initiative. Then a third one was discussed and placed, and so on. Soon, relative priorities among the original group of *must do/nows* began to emerge. A cluster grew of the most important initiatives, and another cluster formed just below. The second cluster was still important, but not quite as important as the first group. And a third cluster, less important than the first two (but all still *must do's*), soon emerged.

How are these new clusters formed? As a cluster gets too large, it can be subdivided by asking whether a particular initiative belongs in the top half or the bottom half of the cluster. Eventually, like an amoeba, the cluster separates into two. In this way it's possible to create finer and finer gradations until you have a reasonable hierarchy of initiatives.

In my experience it's usually enough to subdivide until you arrive at quartiles. Four groups are sufficient to determine which tranches of projects will be funded under four categories of resource scenarios: poor, good, better, and best. By deferring the funding discussion and using clusters to establish priorities, the team can far more easily, efficiently, and effectively discharge one of its chief responsibilities in a way that no other group in the organization can.

Each of the CPG company's initiatives was discussed. Not one was challenged as to its very existence. The question was never whether to kill an individual initiative. Instead, a much easier and much more relevant question was discussed: In terms of relative importance, which cluster of initiatives on the wall does the initiative we're discussing now belong with? Should it be among the most important at the top of the chart? Or is it important, but not as important as that top group? Could it be deferred and started soon, or is it as urgent as the ones in this group? Each initiative is benchmarked against the others—nothing stands on its own. And each initiative gradually takes its place among the others along the critical dimensions of importance and urgency.

It's All Relative

As I've suggested, the company's current situation determines how the SMT combines or sequences the three questions about an initiative: (1) Does this team own it? (2) How important is it relative to the others? (3) How urgent is it relative to the others? The company may already have prioritized by importance but now needs to decide on timing. Or, facing a crippling proliferation of initiatives, it may need to tame issues of both timing and importance right away. Regardless of how it proceeds, the important thing is to harness the underlying principles and significant advantages this approach offers for successfully completing what can otherwise be a very difficult job:

- **Clustering in relative categories is much easier and ultimately more productive than rank ordering.** Absolutely and precisely rank ordering initiatives is virtually impossible. Think, for example, of discussions of the relative intelligence of kids in a classroom (especially now that we recognize many different kinds of intelligence). You might not be able to rigidly rank order the students, but you can see that Kevin is about as smart as Sanjay and Hassan and that Greta, David, and Tom are all somewhat less intelligent and that Iris, Bruce, and Lucia are among the most intelligent of all. And at the end of the day, such clusters are just as actionable as forced rankings while being much faster and easier to execute.

- **The secret lies in fuzzy logic.** The reasoning behind bucketing initiatives this way is roughly analogous to applying *fuzzy logic*—an idea that first appeared in mathematics for situations in which the reasoning is approximate. Fuzzy logic subsequently found its way into many industrial and consumer applications, such as autofocus cameras and washers, where the system acts on the basis of ranges of conditions, not absolute values. Rather than an attempt at false precision, the fuzzy logic of the initiatives prioritization conversation is a series of pairwise comparisons. For example, consider that *warm* doesn't typically have to be a precisely defined term but a condition somewhere between *hot* and *cold*. Even without a thermometer, we can usually tell whether a given bucket of water is hotter or colder than another. Similarly, it's easy for the SMT to get a sense of whether a given initiative is more or less critical than another if it's a question of clustering it in group A or group B. The grouping of initiatives proceeds on the basis of approximations, with neither absolute values for inclusion in a particular group nor absolute ranks for the initiatives within a group.

Fuzzy logic applies to time too. Conversations about the timing of initiatives often attempt an artificial precision, forcing participants to assign each initiative to a start date of 30, 60, 90, or 120 days out. As with rank ordering, such a procedure takes a tremendous amount of effort, entails a lot of frustration, and often makes little progress. What the group really needs to decide is the relative urgency of the initiatives: *now*, *soon*, or *later*.

- **It's not rocket science—and doesn't need to be.** This approach doesn't even have the algorithmic rigor of genuine fuzzy logic in appliances. But it does acknowledge and circumvent the impossibility that plagues what, in my experience, is the method of almost every manager when facing the problem of prioritization: taking a list of initiatives and trying to rank them based on quantitative factors, and trying to force decimal-point precision into business cases where one can have, at best, educated guesses. False precision is doomed to failure, and the simple expedient of bucketing initiatives into quartiles can break the team free of the rigid logic of rank ordering or metrics-based approaches.

- **The left hand learns what the right hand is doing.** Through the prereading and subsequent discussions, the members of the SMT gain a detailed understanding of what's going on throughout the organization. Just as the vision conversations provide them with a common view of the world and the company from a high-level perspective, these conversations provide them with a common perspective on what the company is doing to drive the achievement of its objectives. In both cases, the result is greater alignment, including a common framework for the hundreds of decisions they make in the course of doing their jobs.

By giving up the chimera of rank ordering and addressing the relative—as opposed to the absolute—merits of initiatives, the CEO and the SMT can transform one of the most frustrating tasks they face into one of the most productive and rewarding. Using similar techniques, they can do the same with a related conversation, the one about integrating their initiatives into powerful and precisely aimed instruments of strategy.

Hitting the Bull's-Eye: Making Initiatives Work Together

Beyond the issues of importance and urgency, there is an additional critical question to be asked of initiatives: Are they focused in a way that will provide the maximum contribution to the major strategic objectives that the organization hopes to achieve? Those objectives are the organization's big, short-term aspirations (as opposed to the longer-term vision), and they usually involve hitting some specific quantitative targets over a specific time period, usually a year or two.

Whereas the prioritization discussion is designed to determine which initiatives are important and how urgent they are, the integration discussion is designed to test their impact against a known set of desired outcomes. Then, if necessary, the portfolio of initiatives can be reconfigured to maximize the initiatives' collective impact on those outcomes.

Once again, the SMT is the ideal venue for the task. The people in various functions or groups who own individual initiatives are often focused on a narrow set of outcomes relevant to their immediate areas of responsibility. The SMT is focused on a much broader set of outcomes—the company's strategic objectives—and is looking to drive overall progress toward them and is well positioned to undertake the fully cross-functional alignment and optimization of initiatives that is required.

Although I will be describing a process that I've found extremely helpful in guiding the discussion of initiative integration, my point once again is not to advocate one process over another but to encourage you to embrace the process's central principle: articulate and tightly link groups of initiatives to specific outcomes for maximum impact.

The process begins with a prereading, a book containing brief descriptions of the initiatives that the organization is considering committing to. So the book does not contain all the possible initiatives (like the CPG company's 110 projects) but a much shorter list, starting with the *must do/nows* and then adding the *must do/soons* and, potentially, the *should do/nows* that have emerged from the prioritization process.

For the meeting itself, I place large sheets of paper with images of archery-style targets on the wall. Each has an inner ring—the bull's-eye—and two additional concentric rings. The top of each sheet is labeled with one of the company's major strategic objectives.

For example, for a technology company, the objectives for the coming year were

- Increase gross margins by 14 percent.
- Improve customer satisfaction to 95 percent.
- Increase unit share of our core market by 10 percent.
- Cut new product introduction cycle time by 40 days.

The SMT opened the discussion by choosing an initiative chosen from the prereading: "Create a council of critical customers to meet directly with product engineering during early stage of product development." The group members then discussed which of the four critical targets the initiative should go on and how close to the center to place it—bull's-eye, second ring, or outer ring—depending on whether it directly drove the desired outcome, had a close relationship but wasn't aimed directly at the outcome, or had a tangential role.

It was agreed that a council of critical customers would certainly boost customer satisfaction because products would be more closely tuned to customer needs when they were first introduced. But it was also agreed that the initiative, designed specifically to make the most important customers happier, might not affect the broader base of customers who used the company's products in a wide array of applications. So a Post-it with the initiative title was placed on the second ring, not the bull's-eye of the customer satisfaction target. It was also agreed that the initiative might positively affect new product introduction cycle time, but only tangentially. That is, it would have some impact, but it wouldn't clearly drive a significant number of those forty days out of the process. So this initiative was also placed on the outer ring of the new product cycle time target.

Sometimes an initiative doesn't hit any ring on any of the targets and ends up on a flip chart on the side of the room. That's not to say that the initiative isn't important—its relative importance has likely already been established, and though it might not significantly affect the outcome on any strategic objective, it is still going to be pursued. For example, one of the critical initiatives for the upcoming year might be the rollout of a new module of the HR system—a *must do/now* that will take up significant resources even though it won't directly drive any of the strategic outcomes. The important thing is that the entire SMT acknowledges its importance, understands that it will not drive any strategic outcomes, and still signs off on keeping it a top priority. Imagine the down-the-road discussions both the senior vice president of HR and the chief information officer may potentially avoid as a result of this five-minute interaction alone.

However, most initiatives, like the customer council proposal discussed here, end up somewhere on a target, even though typically not aimed at any bull's-eye but indirectly related to one or more outcomes and tangential to one or two more.

The substance of the prioritization and timing exercise lies in the discussion of each initiative in comparison to the others. But the "aha" moment in the integration discussion typically occurs only after most or all of the Post-its have been distributed among the targets. That's when the team can step back and visually survey how well or badly the entire portfolio of initiatives is linked to the company's big strategic objectives.

Then the question before the SMT is this: Are we doing what we need to do to achieve our objectives, and are the initiatives placed on each objective's target close enough to the center of the target to make that outcome occur? If the answer is yes, great. The team can move on to the next objective. If the answer is no, the team asks how it can merge, reposition, supplement, or create new initiatives to achieve the desired outcomes.

If an objective has few initiatives assigned to it, the team is either assuming that the company will achieve it through business as usual or it is clear that the team needs to devise or revise initiatives to put behind it. An objective with several initiatives in the second and third rings but none in the bull's-eye may indicate that the company is approaching that objective only obliquely and needs to aim its initiatives more accurately. Or the team may find several related initiatives ranging across targets that could be folded together or better coordinated—for example, in terms of time—for higher impact.

Great organizations have both the prioritization conversations and the integration conversations regularly. (I've seen them done separately or together, and I've seen prioritization precede integration and the reverse.) The point is to have the SMT discuss the importance of initiatives relative to each other, how they tie into organizational objectives, and how to make sure that a manageable number are being launched at any given time. The team recognizes that an enormous amount of activity and discussion must take place across organizational boundaries but that hierarchical structures don't lend themselves to the management of initiatives across the organization. Just as the organization chart doesn't describe who really makes decisions, it doesn't begin to suggest the scale and the necessity of this cross-organizational effort.

Despite the two-decimal-point, five-year projections required by some business case and budgeting cycles, the best way to manage key strategic initiatives is through these critical conversations:

- Sort out which initiatives are most important, now.
- Decide which initiatives will be resourced if and when various funding levels are available.
- Determine which initiatives, even though not being launched immediately, will be forming the next wave.
- Make sure that the appropriate number and level of initiatives are positioned to drive the most important outcomes, or that disparate initiatives are integrated to hit closer to the bull's-eyes of critical strategic objectives.

Countless times when I've finished the first stage of the target exercise, with the initiatives scattered across the targets, I've seen the CEO or a functional leader step up and say: "The year hasn't started and we've already admitted, in effect, that we won't make our goals. All right, people, let's figure out how to really move the needle on the commitments we've made." That's when you know you're off to a great conversation—a conversation that the SMT is well positioned to conduct and that fully leverages the unique capabilities of the group.

What remains? The only thing that ultimately counts: successful execution. No matter how well prioritized or how tightly integrated, initiatives will produce disappointing results if they aren't executed successfully. In my experience, initiatives usually fall short not because they are bad ideas or because people are inept, but because the internal resources on which they depend have not been adequately identified, discussed, and committed in advance of implementation.

Here, too, the SMT has a unique opportunity. No group is better positioned to weigh resource requirements and make sure that those resources will flow from the places they reside in the organization to the places where they are needed to make an initiative a reality. Yet in most organizations the conversation about execution rarely goes beyond budgetary considerations or the confines of the often misapplied business case process. The next chapter discusses how to remedy that.

CHAPTER 10

Move from "*Should* We Do This?" to "*How* Do We Do This?"

Jim Noble's career as a technology strategist and chief information officer (CIO) has taken him into the boardrooms of some of the world's largest corporations. He has been CIO at Altria; managing director, Global Technology, at Merrill Lynch; and head of IT strategy for BP and General Motors. He was the inaugural CIO after the merger of AOL and Time Warner. His current role has him serving as senior vice president of IT and Business Services for Talisman Energy, a Calgary-based oil and gas company. As a young man, Jim was part of a much different kind of team—the pit crew for Jackie Stewart, the legendary Scottish racing driver. Jim's entire adult career has been spent as a critical member of the leadership engine at some of the world's largest corporations. This has given him a great deal of insight into another of the highest and best uses of a senior management team (SMT)—determining what he calls *doability*.

"When the Talisman leadership team gets together to consider a business case, we don't challenge the numbers, say, for a $1 billion capital investment," he says. "That's already been decided by the CEO, CFO, and the relevant executives. Instead, we talk about the ability of the organization to accommodate it. It's sort of like corporate air traffic control. It requires the intellect of everyone in the room because no one person knows all the subtle things going on in all of the functions. You're expected to contribute down your line of expertise, to listen for doability issues in your domain. It's demanded of you, and it's the best I've ever seen."

It All Depends: Why Initiatives Fail

At Talisman the SMT members aren't determining if Talisman should do something—that decision has most often already been made. They're determining if they can do it, and how to do it within the context of competing corporate priorities. In determining this doability—or what I think of as *dependency management*—the task is to ensure that each function of the business is prepared and committed to support the successful completion of strategically important activities and initiatives.

The SMT business case review process offers a unique opportunity to do just that: identify, discuss, and commit resources to flow across organizational boundaries to where they are required. All the functions and business areas are represented on the SMT by executives with the authority to commit any of the resources of the organization. Other than the Office of the CEO, the SMT is the most senior, most compact group where the whole organization comes together.

But for most companies, doability is not the focal point of those stage-managed meetings where the senior team nominally approves a business case. In the example in Chapter One, the problem for CIO Dave with the plant expansion in China wasn't that the proposal he spent the weekend reading was a bad idea.

The fact that it had made it as far as the SMT suggests that the idea was quite likely something the company ought to do, and by the time it got to Dave it was clearly something that the CEO and his kitchen cabinet had already decided to do.

The real problems arise when a business case blows through the meeting room and is agreed to without clarity about what the participants are actually signing up for—which resources each function will ultimately have to supply in order to deliver on the proposal as it actually gets implemented. Because the team that developed the business case can't possibly be aware of all the alternative activities potentially drawing on the same resources, conflicts may not surface until a project is well under way. In fact, most business case templates focus more on the direct costs and resources under the control of the initiative itself than they do on the costs and resources assumed to be available but carried on the budgets of other functions.

Failure to properly identify and manage dependencies is one of the primary reasons initiatives fail. When initiatives enter the arena of executional reality, they begin to run into internal resource constraints—organizational frictions that one CEO calls *rub points*. These frictions wear away at the ability of the organization to achieve the goals of the initiatives. The failure to aggressively identify rub points up front and to bring the individual and collective ability of the SMT to bear on eliminating those rub points leads to this executional failure.

It has always struck me as surprising that business case processes that require detailed budget projections going out three, five, or even ten years often fail to address basic questions of execution. Labor costs for different types of workers are calculated, but the availability of HR Department personnel to hire those workers is simply assumed. Desktop software implementation schedules are planned months in advance, but the fact that the field rollout coincides with the scheduled release of a major new product doesn't necessarily surface. "When you're proposing SAP for supply chain, for example, you obviously work it with the lower-level people in the business," says Noble. "But they don't know that there's a pending merger, a pending acquisition, or a pending disposal. So with the best will in the world and the best of intentions, you will come forward with something that at face value seems doable. But only the chief executive's team knows whether or not it really is doable."

Many companies and their teams believe that they are managing those kinds of dependencies, but in my experience they often do so after the fact, when an initiative has already run into trouble. For example, after much thought and consultation with close advisers, the CEO of an industrial company decided to launch a major, enterprise-wide training initiative. It was an expensive undertaking, but the projected long-term benefits seemed well worth it. An experienced executive was recruited from another company known for best-in-class corporate learning and development. This new executive spent six months designing a state-of-the-art program and building her business case. The initiative was presented to the Senior Management Team. No one could deny that it was a good idea. The CEO had already established it as a priority with the board. Funds had been set aside in the budget, and the program was cutting edge. The business case sailed through without a hitch.

But once rollout began, members of the SMT discovered that implementing the training curriculum would mean shutting selected operations for days at a time while workers attended their new courses. The training protocols required pulling key managers from their jobs to attend train-the-trainer sessions, which were all being held at the new corporate headquarters training center and involved additional days of travel for many managers. Hours of prework were required for each worker attending the training. Already stretched field administrative personnel were assumed to be taking on support responsibilities for training logistics—from room setup to IT support—at each training location. Although the direct costs to the training department for trainers, curriculum development, and the building of a new corporate training center had been estimated to decimal point precision, none of this incremental time had been included in the business case, nor had the temporary drop in productivity. The business case team had limited the indirect impact calculation to the actual classroom days of individuals attending the training sessions.

There was an uproar—to the extent that you can have an uproar amid the thick carpeting and wood paneling of the executive suite of a Fortune 50 company. Members of the SMT made it clear that their functions and business areas simply could not afford the time and disruption the new training and development program would cost in practice. Too often, that is the point at which real dependency management begins, only after there is enormous pushback or an initiative is sinking under its own weight. And that's precisely what occurred in this situation.

The CEO felt that he had to back his new head of learning and development and her initiative, because it was something he had put into motion, approved, and taken to his board. But he knew he had a business to run, and he had rarely seen this level of unified pushback from his three business unit heads. He told them, "We agreed on these action plans. But you've got two choices. Step up to the resources and get it done, or we'll have to change the action plan. I'm not going to sit here and say we're going to get something done and then not get it done because of resources. That's not an option."

At the end of the day, the company ended up reducing the action plan. The ambitious training and development program was scaled back. By the end of the year, the recently hired head of corporate learning and development had retired.

The particular company in this example is actually extremely good at prioritizing initiatives at the beginning of the strategy cycle, and like most companies it builds resource requirements into the business case at lower levels of planning. What its business case process doesn't seek to do, and the SMT didn't do during the approval process, is aggressively identify and root out these potential conflicts in advance. That happens largely after initiatives are under way and they hit rub points. Then the sponsor of each affected initiative individually approaches functional heads and other leaders who have problems with implementation and in sequential, bilateral fashion seeks to work out the conflicts. As the CEO says, "We work it out off-line."

Unless, as in the case of the corporate learning initiative, the problems are too big to work out and the initiative blows up. Jim Noble's air traffic control analogy is apt in this case. How do you prevent the planes from colliding, rather than having to sort out the wreckage afterward? By managing dependencies.

Putting on the Brakes: The Value of Parochialism

The experience of a major European car manufacturer provides a case study of the benefits to be gained from leaders who tenaciously represent their domains, despite the pressure to take a holistic view. I have masked certain technical details along with the identity of the company in order to tell this story, but it's a compelling example of the virtues of parochialism, of taking the narrow view—the prerequisite for managing dependencies.

By 2000, this company, like most automakers, had been building computing systems into its cars for more than a decade, following GM's lead in the late 1980s. As the company looked forward to its next-generation vehicle, the leader of its Engineering Group, with the backing of the general managers, decided to pursue an aggressive new design philosophy in the redesign of the next-generation platform. The then current model had seventeen major microprocessors distributed throughout the car, each of which controlled a separate subsystem such as brakes, engine, audio, HVAC, and so on. Future designs would combine these into three central processors, with each of the three controlling multiple systems and providing redundancy in case any of them failed. According to the business case, the new design would generate cost, maintenance, and manufacturing advantages over the competition. Moreover, a major software company was prepared to invest significantly in developing the master processors and the operating system to run them.

The overall Engineering Team was composed of the lead engineer for each subsystem, much as SMTs are composed of representatives from each of a company's functions. The Brakes Group, however, was putting up tremendous resistance to the new design philosophy—so much so in fact that my firm was called in to help design a process to get everyone on the same page.

Although the general manager and the leader of the Engineering Team said that they wanted us to act as honest brokers, they understandably were hoping that the Brakes Group would be brought to see the light or, at least, would reluctantly align around the new design, which was an important element of the emerging corporate strategy. In any case, we structured the workshops to make sure that all points of view could be expressed and that there would be no predetermined outcome.

The workshops themselves unfolded like *12 Angry Men,* the unforgettable film in which the character played by Henry Fonda patiently and methodically persuades eleven other jurors to reconsider their rush to convict a young man who is on trial for murder. Like the Fonda character, the leader of the Brakes Group began the first two-day workshop as a minority of one, and between sessions he was widely criticized for being parochial and territorial. Why stand in the way of a clearly advantageous and futuristic redesign, the others wanted to know. Nevertheless he refused to concede. Further, his views certainly represented those of his people; discussions with his subordinates in the Brakes Group made it clear that they unanimously supported him.

Their argument was compelling. They said, in effect:

The Brakes Group is responsible for making sure our automobiles stop, under a wide range of conditions and scenarios. We control everything from the rubber coating of the brake pedals to the abrasives on the brake disks. End to end. And our cars stop, reliably, when they are supposed to. Now you are proposing to merge the braking system's microprocessor into a processor where the code and functioning of the brakes are intertwined with those of unrelated systems. The front end of our system will go into a box we do not control and continue on to the back end of our system. If you do that, we won't be able to tell you definitively and confidently that the braking system will work every time. And if it doesn't work we won't be able to tell you why. We will no longer be able to take responsibility for the car stopping, which is what we're here for.

The people who developed the case for the three-microprocessor design were playing by the rules of the business case—Is this proposal a good idea from the point of view of corporate strategy? They had gathered technical information from engineers in the Brakes Group about how to design the microprocessors and software, but they had never asked for the Brakes Group's opinion about whether it was a good idea from their parochial point of view.

The tide began to turn. The other Engineering subgroups began to see that they, too, would be unable to vouch for the functioning of their subsystems—and yet in the event of failure they would likely be held accountable. After lengthy one-on-one and group discussions, the point of view of the Brakes Group prevailed. The company decided to retain dedicated microprocessors not only for the brakes but for several other critical subsystems.

Flash forward ten years. Today's premium-class cars may contain as many microprocessor-based electronic control units as the Airbus A380. And just as *fly-by-wire* technology is ubiquitous in passenger aircraft, *drive-by-wire* is now a reality in many cars, which today contain and must execute close to 100 million lines of software code. The sheer size and complexity of today's code make it extremely difficult to get to the root cause of a malfunction in a subsystem. When subsystems are merged, the problem becomes almost impossible to solve with finality and assurance, as the Brakes Group was, in essence, arguing.

Imagine what might have happened if the automaker in our example, back in those relatively early days of computer-controlled cars, had installed central processors in its next-generation model. These processors could have worked out well, or they could have proven to be a disaster, given the relatively primitive tools for software development and testing available at the time. But this automaker didn't take that risk, largely because the leader of the Brakes Group was doing the job he was best suited for: evaluating the implications of the engineering strategy from the point of view of his area of expertise. He had spent a lifetime designing, testing, and improving brake systems. If forced to take the holistic view he might have reluctantly conceded—or ritually agreed—that the strategy's competitive advantages in terms of costs, manufacturing, and maintenance seemed like a good idea. Instead, he took the point of view of his function and stuck to it, even though it was like standing in front of a moving train, which through his persistence he was able to stop.

The actions of the head of the Brakes Group represent an extreme situation. No organization could function if everyone behaved with such intransigence all the time. But the case emphatically makes the point that having team members represent their functions and their expertise can yield invaluable benefits in terms of doability, even at the very high level of strategy and policy, where it's too often assumed that what is called for is the generalist's perspective and executives are routinely asked to take off their functional hats at the beginning of the discussion.

The SMT is precisely the forum in which such functional points of view should be thrashed out. Not that every SMT discussion should be totally functional. Far from it. But in an effort to be inclusive, to be holistic, and to form cooperative teams, many organizations no longer know how to allow their senior executives to publicly take a purely internalized, parochial view when necessary—to weigh in from an entirely Finance or HR or Marketing or Sales or Operations perspective. With the perceived need for executives to lift themselves above their boxes in the organization chart and see the bigger picture, presenting one's own smaller picture has become politically incorrect. And the result is that one of the most valuable things a team member can do goes unexploited.

The American Red Cross: Managing Dependencies at the Speed of Disaster

Gail McGovern, the president and CEO of the American Red Cross, assumed leadership of this iconic organization at a particularly tough time. In 2008, when she was chosen from among 170 candidates, the institution's reputation had been tarnished by the response to Hurricane Katrina and by a string of leadership scandals. A thousand employees, most of them in the Red Cross headquarters, had recently been laid off. A series of floods in the Midwest one week before she took over had seriously depleted resources. Fundraising was going badly, and she entered office facing an operating deficit of $209 million.

A longtime corporate executive, McGovern had previously run AT&T's consumer markets division, a $26 billion business with 40,000 employees, and had been president of Distribution and Services at Fidelity Investments. She had also spent a half dozen years teaching at Harvard Business School. In less than two years, during one of the most difficult economic periods in American history, she and her team turned the Red Cross's $209 million operating deficit into a surplus, restored the institution's reputation, and expanded its broad range of services while cutting costs.

The scale and diversity of those services are enormous. With nearly 700 local chapters, 35,000 employees, and half a million volunteers, the Red Cross must respond to some 70,000 disasters a year—everything from apartment fires to floods to earthquakes. It is also the largest supplier of blood and blood products in the United States and provides extensive community services and educational programs.

Given those diverse obligations, the organization runs in two strikingly different gears—business-as-usual and crisis mode. Business as usual proceeds in the weekly, quarterly, annual, and multiyear planning rhythm familiar to most large enterprises, for-profit and nonprofit alike. But faced with a crisis, the organization shifts into the urgent rhythm demanded by the almost instantaneous, life-and-death decisions Gail and her team need to make. Aside from other emergency response organizations and the military in combat, few organizations experience the fierce immediacy that the American Red Cross does in a disaster.

When disasters strike, the members of the Red Cross leadership team not only go into crisis mode but also physically go into the organization's Disaster Operations Center, designed expressly for such crises.

"The room actually is like Mission Control," says Peggy Dyer, chief marketing officer, whose experience includes ten years at Allstate Insurance Company and stints representing such brands as Citigroup, Sara Lee, and Quaker Oats. "There is a huge table, probably forty feet long—with microphones, big screens, Internet connections—and people outside of Washington, D.C., call in on the telephone. Most of the discussion and decisions take place with everyone, out in the open. You might have people who are on the ground in Haiti, for example, participating in the discussion, and anybody can weigh in."

With all the parts moving at once, it is a management team on fast-forward. "During a disaster, I cannot tell you how fast and furious this all is," says McGovern. "We knock off decisions so quickly and I go pretty much into directive mode."

A particular disaster response is like a critical initiative, only at warp speed, and a vivid reminder that dependencies matter. The speed and compression with which the Red Cross team manages dependencies in a crisis—and the immediacy of the consequences—make it a particularly instructive example for companies, bringing into sharp focus management team issues that often get lost in the far slower business rhythms of many for-profit organizations. Doability comes unavoidably to the fore, and success in addressing it is directly measured in the numbers of people living or dying, instead of the abstract outcomes that are rarely measured or followed up on in many business settings.

"In my former life in for-profits, when people would get crazed during discussions, I would say 'relax, we're not saving lives here,'" says McGovern. "But when we're sitting in a room and making decisions that are affecting 1.3 million people in Haiti who are living in tents and under tarps, I don't get to say that anymore."

When Hurricane Earl, a category 4 storm, was threatening the East Coast of the United States in 2010, McGovern, her top team, and other key personnel convened in the Disaster Operations Center. The dependencies were many and those responsible for specific functions could make invaluable contributions. McGovern ticks off some of the key players who were in the room and their responsibilities: "My head of government relations is there because five states are threatened and we will have to coordinate with their governors. My auditor sits there because there's huge opportunity for fraud as we send supplies here, there, and everywhere. My finance guy sits there because he's got to see that this disaster doesn't take us under financially. My head of development is there because we're calling for in-kind donations and financial donations. And of course my head of disaster operations is sitting there because he orchestrates everything."

Although the team conducts numerous tabletop exercises to prepare themselves for various emergency scenarios, each disaster is unique, creating unique dependencies. For example, for a disaster in the Americas, like the Haiti earthquake, the immediate fundraising effort may be less difficult than it would be in the case of a similarly devastating earthquake in a faraway country, to which many U.S. donors might be less sympathetic. In each of those cases, the dependencies to be worked out between, say, the head of Finance and the head of Development would differ. Is the fundraising likely to bring enough money to cover the scale of the organization's commitment? If not, to what extent can or should the organization tap into its reserve resources to cover the costs? How large can the commitment be without endangering the organization's viability?

In managing dependencies during a disaster, the team is not acting purely in the mode of Mission Control—simply providing a "go" or "no go" for each of the organization's functional areas. Nor are the members operating as Knights of the Round Table, although everything they are doing is for the greater good of the organization and its mission of service. They are operating in their areas of specialization, no question, but they are also coordinating with other functions by communicating what they believe they can commit to.

What they are not doing, however, is acting as though their role is to be the "nine wise people of the Red Cross," collectively deliberating on each decision and attempting a consensus style of decision making. Decisions are made either by individuals around the table or passed up to McGovern. Team members are there to provide supporting data and context to individual decisions and to coordinate activity among themselves—all within the rapid-fire environment of life-and-death decisions as a disaster is unfolding.

What makes acting in this situation even more complicated is that it's impossible for the Red Cross to know what its future portfolio of emergencies will look like. It just knows that disasters are both inevitable and unpredictable and that the organization's success depends in part on the ability to accommodate arising disasters both in relation to each other and in relation to the portfolio of initiatives undertaken in the organization's business-as-usual mode—initiatives in information technology, blood services, marketing, fundraising, and other areas.

Most companies don't face nearly so complicated a challenge. To dramatically improve dependency management at the very top of your organization, you don't need to somehow simulate an emergency-response situation or, like the European automaker, conduct a contentious workshop. The best place to start is to make some clear and explicit changes to one of the most critical yet neglected tools at your disposal—the business case process. In this process, fundamental questions of doability, dependencies, and execution should, but rarely do, come together. Transforming this process can help the SMT transition to much more effective dependency management.

Going from "Should" to "How"

As we've seen, positioning the SMT as the decision-making authority at the pinnacle of the business case process is a sham at most companies. The reality is that decisions have essentially been made by the time they get to the senior team, having been all but decided by the accountable executive, with critical sign-offs acquired along the way. Yet the near-universal use of the SMT for final review and some form of sign-off on business cases goes unchallenged and unchanged.

Making that process useful begins with a frank recognition of several major shortcomings of the business case process, all of which are contributing factors to the failure to address dependencies:

- **Business cases are inherently one-sided selling documents.** Whether business cases are being presented to the senior team or to a single executive, they have a glaring weakness: They are written and put forward by people who want the answer to be yes. The head of manufacturing who proposes a major plant expansion has an inherent stake in the outcome. Resources, and the power and prestige that come with them, are on the line. Although the risks of the proposed initiative will be considered in the business case, the authors may discount those risks and downplay alternative courses of action.

Further, the sponsors of the business case—especially if they are top executives—understandably believe in the merit of their ideas.

The tendency to sell a business case may be a natural response to the situation rather than a well-planned tactic. In their *Harvard Business Review* article "Delusions of Success: How Optimism Undermines Executive Decision Making," Dan Lovallo and Daniel Kahneman explore cognitive biases that lead people to overemphasize projects' potential benefits, underestimate the likely costs, and create success scenarios while ignoring the possibility of mistakes.[1] In addition, most how-to books on the subject focus on how to be persuasive. For example, the product description for one of Amazon.com's top titles on this topic—*How to Build a Business Case*, by Clifford Earl—says "this book is for technical and business professionals who must persuade others that their project should be approved and funded."

- **The business case process is dominated by the finance perspective.** Whether considered as one-off decisions or as part of a series of investments constrained by overall corporate spending, business cases lean heavily on financial analysis. But the success of any individual initiative often depends not just on operating or capital expenditures, but on the availability of specific resources at the functional level. Imagine how odd it would seem if the process were dominated by the HR viewpoint and focused entirely on people, not dollars. Or if it had an IT focus and the orientation was toward technology assets, or a legal point of view and the whole thing turned on an axis of legal issues. Obviously, it makes no sense to frame a business case in terms of one function, yet in most companies the process remains primarily in the realm of financial data on spreadsheets rather than in a real discussion of doability. The business case process as currently practiced typically overemphasizes the allocation of financial resources, and it is not optimized to effectively balance the allocation of other critical, constrained resources of the organization.

- **Individual business cases are typically considered serially.** As a result, the finite functional resources not already absorbed by business as usual may already have been allocated to other initiatives. The proposals that get the lion's share of funding are not necessarily optimized around the best cases but rather those that come at fortunate times in the approval cycle. Later initiatives, no matter how worthy, may be postponed, underfunded, or simply impossible to accomplish as planned. There is, in effect, no bottom-up portfolio view of how the finite resources of each corporate function (such as IT, HR, Marketing, or Sales) will be spread over all the various initiatives within a planning horizon.

Missing from these finance-dominated, serially considered selling documents are answers to the fundamental questions of doability:

- What are the significant nonfinancial resources the organization will require to implement this business case, and will the initiative run into constraints on any of those resources?
- What resources beyond the immediate scope and control of the sponsoring organization will be required, and is this initiative baked into those organizations' plans and objectives?
- How does this business case fit into the opportunities that have been approved already or are in the pipeline for approval later?
- Does this project need to be done now, and what are the alternatives for either scaling it down or delaying it if resources are constrained?

When these questions are answered, functional and business leaders can affirm their commitment to do the things their groups will need to do to have the initiative succeed.

As we've seen, top executives are the first to admit that the senior team meetings at which business cases are nominally approved are largely charades. In fact, they say, the real value of the final approval meeting is to force the sponsor to get the relevant executives on board before the meeting actually occurs. As one top executive puts it, "Only a fool would go into the final meeting with a proposal that hadn't already been wired for approval."

Having the business case wired before the final meeting isn't inherently bad. In fact some executives see the role of the final meeting as having two purposes: pro forma approval of major expenditures before they go to the board, and making sure the sponsors and authors of business cases have dotted the *i*'s and crossed the *t*'s. But these two outcomes are hardly worth the time expended on these sessions. More important, wiring an outcome is a far cry from managing dependencies, no matter how many hours staff people at lower levels have put in to provide technical assistance and advice in the construction of the case. As Jim Noble points out, those staff people simply cannot know everything that is going on both in other functions and at the highest levels of the company.

These shortcomings in the business case process result in two sins by the top-management team: one of commission and one of omission. First, the team poorly discharges one of its chief responsibilities—the optimal allocation of company resources. That means all company resources, not just dollars, across initiatives. Second, in the final meeting, where representatives from all critical functions are present to review business cases, the team misses the opportunity to align the organization around the success of an initiative by managing its dependencies.

But by making a few simple but critical changes in the way that business cases are prepared and discussed, leadership teams can make the final consideration of a proposal into a powerful tool for resource allocations and cross-organizational alignment:

- Set the strategic dimension of the business case in the context of the team members' conversations about their common view of the world and the company and their prioritization of initiatives.

- Set the business case in the context of the cases that have been previously approved and those that are likely to arise in the future.
- Create templates that require answers to the fundamental questions of doability, including critical resource dependencies as well as risk assumptions.
- Use the final SMT review meeting to probe those dependencies and assumptions—with each member representing his or her function rather than the team acting as a single executive entity.
- Gain commitments from each team member to deliver the critical resources identified, with the team understanding the trade-offs involved and potential downstream implications.
- Recast ownership of initiatives arising from strategically important business cases to the SMT as a whole, with both individual and collective responsibilities and consequences, instead of viewing the sponsoring function as the sole owner of the initiative going forward.

In the transformed process being proposed here, the CEO sets the doability conversation in the contexts of the ongoing conversations about vision and priorities and insists that team members keep their functional hats on to tease out issues around dependencies and implementation. Instead of asking broad sweeping questions such as, "So, what do we all think?" the CEO homes in on specifics, asking each of the representatives around the table if he or she is prepared to commit the specific resources required to make the proposal succeed.

For example, the question is not only whether the head of HR liked the proposal but also, and more importantly, whether HR is ready to deliver the personnel resources needed to make the plan succeed. That means the head of HR must consider how each of the required finite resources of her function has been distributed, or is likely to be distributed, over the entire portfolio of initiatives in the current planning horizon. That drives the portfolio view down into an area where the business case previously never went—to questions of dependency management and the allocation of resources.

At Talisman Energy the process for addressing doability rests on a culture that demands of each individual in the meeting a keen awareness of dependencies and an obligation to speak up. A more formal approach involves a business case template in a binder with tabs for each function or business area. Leaders of each area turn to their individual tabs and see exactly what they are being asked to commit to in terms of resources. If someone cannot make a critical commitment, the business case might be rejected or rewritten, or the project might be postponed until all the required resources are available; this would not be worked out off-line while the initiative proceeds, or worse, after it breaks down. And when indirect resources—resources required by the initiative but residing in other budgets—are left unidentified, then initiative owners should have no expectation that those resources will be made available during the life of the project.

Instead of being a time-wasting occasion of perfunctory agreement, the business case discussion becomes an opportunity for surfacing critical dependencies and achieving cross-functional alignment around a course of action. Team members are no longer simply ratifying something implicitly agreed to before the meeting. They are jump-starting the execution of the initiative, greatly decreasing the likelihood that the initiative will stall later and greatly increasing the likelihood that it will produce tangible results.

By signing off on dependencies as a group, the team is building collective ownership for the successful implementation of the initiative, rather than blessing the launching of a new initiative under the sponsorship of a single member. No other group in the organization—not the kitchen cabinet, the business case team, or any other entity—is better positioned to have this critical conversation and fulfill the essential function of all great staffs: to enable the leader to get things done.

Fixing What's Actually Broken

Asking people to act from their functional points of view is not the antithesis of asking them to be a team. In fact this is part of what being a team means—having each other's backs, making sure initiatives don't falter, and mutually taking responsibility for success. Like the players on a sports team, members of the SMT drive for the greater good by performing their highly specific and interdependent roles, not by having each member play all the positions at once.

Contrast that with the situation in which dependencies are managed largely by the team that builds the business case. Here's how one CEO I interviewed sees it: "Good leadership sets the priorities of the company in making resource allocations to get the job done. So we hardwire the matrix of resources and we say, on behalf of the company as a whole, 'So-and-so has accountability for this. We as a leadership team have agreed to support it, so let's get on with the action plan. If we have a resource problem, we'll work it out.' And if I'm in HR, or I'm in IT, I'm going to support these things because that's what support organizations are there to do."

Dependencies be damned; full speed ahead with the business case! If resource bottlenecks occur later, as is likely when the dependencies haven't been worked out, what happens from a teaming perspective? Does the member of the team with accountability have the right to beat up on the head of HR or the head of IT? How is that going to go over? But doesn't the person who has been given the ball and told to run with it and who has then found himself bogged down in the muck and the mire have a right to resent his peers who aren't coming through? Conversely, do team members have a right to feel that they're being unfairly squeezed by an effort that was poorly planned by its sponsors?

At some point the SMT as a whole will appear to be dysfunctional. But it's not psychological dysfunction, as the behavioralists would have you believe. Fifty shrinks couldn't fix this problem. It's a failure of process, a failure to put the team to one of its highest and best uses, and a failure to have the right conversation. Until your team is having the right conversations—about members' common view of the world, the prioritization and integration of initiatives, and the management of dependencies—you are missing out on the best way to build an effective team: allow it to succeed at the things that it is best suited to do and that also confer the most advantage on the business.

Note

1. Dan Lovallo and Daniel Kahneman, "Delusions of Success: How Optimism Undermines Executive Decision Making," *Harvard Business Review* (July 2003), pp. 56–63.

CHAPTER 11

Tailor Your Portfolio of Teams for Top Performance Now

If I've done my job right, your thinking about the teams around you has come a long way over the past ten chapters. From the discontents of SMT members in the first chapter, we've moved to introducing the portfolio approach to teams and then focused on making the most of the extraordinary asset your Senior Management Team represents. Along the way, four fundamental principles have emerged:

1. **Teams don't decide—executives do.** Teams can provide valuable input, insights, and ideas—they are a critical element of management. Their discussions can surface solutions and provide persuasive points of view. But it's rare that a major decision is actually put in the hands of a team. In some cases the team will be *informed* about a decision that has essentially been made. In cases where the decision has not yet been made and the leader wants input from the team

before proceeding, the team can be *consulted* for its members' perspectives. In still other cases the team may be *responsible* for communicating or implementing the decision under discussion. But all these functions are different from the team *being the decision maker*. Even in those situations where the leader decides to proceed by going with the group consensus, the implicit understanding is that this group decision will lie within an acceptable set of boundaries established by the accountable executive. True group decision making is a rare event in practice because groups don't have accountability. Individuals do.

2. **The SMT shouldn't be considered an all-powerful group at the focal point of all key decisions and processes.** All important issues and decisions don't need to pass in front of the SMT on the path to final disposition. Viewing the SMT as the central decision-making authority is not only simplistic but also the cause of unnecessary tensions, both for the organization at large and for SMT members themselves. Dispelling the myth of the SMT members as the gods on Olympus and recasting them as a unique instance of an ordinary organizational construct—an executive's staff—can be a more powerful transformative tool than years of organizational coaching and team building.

3. **Kitchen cabinets are an inevitable and desirable part of a leader's support system.** When critical decisions must be made, leaders want and need the counsel of trusted advisers. They may form a small core group that gets together regularly, occasionally joined by one or two others, or a leader may choose to get opinions from others one by one. But it's rarely, if ever, the Senior Management Team's meeting as a full group that fulfills this crucial sounding-board function for a CEO. The gap between this reality and the myth of the SMT as the senior decision-making authority can cause dysfunctions often misperceived as behavioral or psychological.

4. **A renewed emphasis on the SMT's alignment functions will give its members more real influence than ever over the course of the business and will reenergize them.** Given their experience and representativeness, the executives on the SMT are ideally suited to address three of the most important responsibilities of senior leadership: helping to set direction, allocating resources, and ensuring effective execution. Through a series of structured conversations, they fulfill each of those responsibilities by, respectively, developing a common view of the world and the company, prioritizing and integrating initiatives, and managing dependencies within and among initiatives to ensure their doability. By focusing their time and energy on the tasks they are best suited for, they will gain clarity about how they can add value *as a team*.

Like many of the leaders I work with, you are no doubt familiar with the issues and challenges of decision making that these four principles speak to. But you may not have systematically addressed those challenges by rethinking the way you maximize the value of the teams around you. And you may be leery of undertaking a far-reaching organizational makeover. In fact, making the transition to a portfolio of teams that suits both your needs as a leader and the needs of the organization usually isn't a massive job. It doesn't require an extensive restructuring of the organization chart, and you don't need a SWAT team of consultants swarming over the organization to implement it.

The basic building blocks already lie near at hand, in the form of structures, core processes, and people. You only need to take what you already have, both the elements laid out in organization charts and process flows and the familiar but probably undocumented ad hoc teams and processes, and build them into an integrated design that works for you and your organization.

Most companies already have some variant of the three naturally occurring types of teams: a kitchen cabinet or some other advisory groups around the leader, an SMT, and a larger group of executives just below it. Decision-making processes exist, both documented and actual. The SMT members are likely already equipped with the experience and competencies required for the highest and best uses of their team. With these resources already in place, you need to do only three things to begin the transition:

- Think through how to reconfigure and coordinate your teams to fit your style.
- Candidly and explicitly tell your staff why you're doing this.
- Jump-start the change by refocusing the SMT and redefining its role.

Thinking It Through

Thinking about how best to use the existing and potential teams in the organization typically takes only a moderate amount of your time, alone or in consultation with a kitchen cabinet, a consultant, or some other adviser.

There is no one best way to configure the teams around you, but there is one overarching principle you should follow: the portfolio must be tailored for you. It must fit your leadership style, your preferred way of making decisions, and your perceptions of what the organization needs to move forward. As we saw in discussing Tom Wilson's makeover of Allstate (in Chapter Five), it's hard to wear a suit cut for someone else. Too often leaders inherit their predecessor's suit—the management structures, processes, and teams that fit the previous leader. New leaders often shorten the sleeves or have the pants taken in a bit, but they rarely custom-tailor the entire suit.

In thinking about the best structure to put into place for yourself, the goal is to ensure two things: that you're getting the input you need to make decisions and that the executives around you have the opportunity to align their points of view and coordinate organizational activities effectively.

As you think about shifting the SMT away from the epicenter of decision making and employing a portfolio of teams,
it's helpful to think of yourself, your advisers and staff, and
the company beyond in terms of a series of concentric circles.
You, the leader, are at the center. Next is the kitchen cabinet
ring—those small groups of trusted internal and external advisers
from whom you seek input before making major decisions. Then
comes the SMT—your staff—with their repurposed functions.
Beyond them is the larger team that you can employ for input,
brainstorming, identifying implementation obstacles, communications, and other broad purposes. And beyond are still more
rings, until you get to the ring of all the employees. Some executives design a model that pushes even further, going outward to
customers and suppliers. Overlaid on these circles are committees
and initiative teams, each of them having a specific purpose, often
an intentionally limited life span, and clear deliverables.

To begin designing this whole ecosystem, think first about
the way in which you actually use your SMT:

- **Determine how much time you actually spend with the
  SMT.** You might be surprised to learn how many hours per
  year you and your executive team are spending meeting with
  each other. When my firm was asked by a Fortune 500 CEO
  to audit the time his SMT members spent together, he was
  shocked at the results. In the prior twelve months these executives had spent forty-three scheduled days meeting together
  or having individuals or teams come to meet with them as
  a group. In addition, the SMT was taking part in larger all-
  officer meetings, sales conferences, town hall meetings, and
  recognition events. "With the senior team spending over
  a quarter of their time meeting with each other," the CEO
  said, "it's a wonder they have time left over to run their
  businesses."
  At the other end of the spectrum, another of my clients had
  major strategic decisions that needed to be made and a host

of critical issues that had not been resolved. The SMT was scheduled to meet for two hours, twice a month. But most of those meetings were consumed with day-to-day operational issues. Too little time was being invested, by anyone, to work through very important problems. The urgent had crowded out the important, and more structured time was needed.

- **Consider the range of issues the SMT addresses.** To get an idea of this, you might review several months' worth of agendas for team meetings. The typical SMT discusses a broad range of issues, from approving budgets and business cases to adjusting medical leave policies and reviewing office space moves—in addition to providing ongoing operational oversight of the business. The question is whether your SMT has the appropriate set of issues coming before it, or whether it has become a catchall for a variety of minor issues and decisions that have no other home and, typically, end up cluttering the agendas of most Senior Management Teams.

- **Clarify what you ask from the SMT.** When you bring issues in front of the SMT, what is the outcome you are seeking? Given the range of issues that the SMT has been dealing with and that it should deal with in the future, what's the role of the group with respect to your decision making around those issues? Are you looking for decisions, consensus, alignment, pushback, operational coordination? And how well does the reality of what you want from them map against what you tell them and the world (through a team charter or the like) that they do?
  Says Steve Loranger, chairman, president, and CEO of ITT, of the need to clarify in advance the status of an issue under discussion by his SMT, "Occasionally, things still get to the top where someone thinks they're making a recommendation, someone else didn't know it was a recommendation, someone thinks we've made a decision, and someone else didn't think we've made a decision. What

is required is a process of communication and preparation before the discussion."

- **Look at some important recent decisions, and think about how those decisions actually happened.** In the course of making each decision, what did you look to your close advisers for and what did you seek from the SMT, subject matter experts, or external advisers? Who really played what part in the process of, say, decisions like acquisitions, big strategic moves, large capital expenditures, business case approvals, and critical hiring decisions?

At the end of this exercise you should have a good foundation for structuring and using the naturally occurring teams around you in a way that works best for you and your organization.

You likely already have a set of trusted advisers, whether constant or shifting, either meeting as a kitchen cabinet or frequently engaged in a set of one-on-one consultations with you. Although these teams and relationships probably aren't documented on your organization chart, it's not a bad idea to put down on paper the people you tend to reach out to on different topics. The key change needed here is that, rather than considering these teams an afterthought, you begin to think of them as what they are—the most important relationships you have.

Most SMTs are made up of the boss's direct reports—the next layer down on the organization chart from the person who is top and center. The roster of your SMT may remain as is or, like Tom Wilson, you may decide to change it. When Wilson went to a new construct for his executive team, he took the opportunity to expand it. Because the team members would be meeting less frequently and on a clearly defined set of issues, he saw a chance to broaden membership to a wider set of executives, knowing that this change wouldn't slow the decision-making process.

The third and larger naturally occurring team can be designated by status—all officers or the SMT plus direct reports, or the like. You may also want to designate some key players you want to be sure to have in that group, regardless of their level, in order to add creativity, insight, or a different perspective to the discussion. You can put the group together along whatever criteria make sense for your style and the company's needs. It's said that Steve Jobs put together the attendee list for his annual Top 100 meeting at Apple by asking himself a question like this: Who are the 99 other people I would take with me to start a new company? His list changed every year.

In parallel with structuring these concentric groups of leaders, you should review your standing committees. Determine which of their tasks can be transferred to clearly defined but limited-duration initiative teams, with fixed purposes, fluid memberships, and end points. There will of course be some standing committees that you must retain—those that are statutory, industry driven, or designed to address regularly recurring issues.

The remaining element is to define a starter set of time-limited initiative teams. You will always have a flexible capacity for other initiative teams as needed and the security of knowing that these time-limited groups will expire when their work is done, thus avoiding organizational bloat. As I'll describe in a moment, the SMT can be engaged in defining this initial group of initiative teams, and so even though you may have a sense of what those teams should be, this can easily remain one of those open issues where SMT input and buy-in are essential.

With a basic structure in hand for your portfolio and key names attached to the key teams—except for the kitchen cabinet, the virtue of which is its flexibility and discretionary status—you're ready to take the next critical step: introducing this new way of working to the organization.

Putting the New Approach into Motion

At this stage you should communicate to your SMT the general outline of what you intend. But you should also share, in depth and in detail, your reasons for undertaking the change. Your people need to understand not only what you're doing but, just as important, why you're doing it.

Think of this as another of those invaluable discussions about things that are rarely talked about because they seem obvious, are considered to be what "everybody knows," or involve elephants in the room. You'll likely find that what seems obvious to some is news to others and that what "everybody knows" differs from person to person. The explicit rationale behind the changes you make in roles, processes, and structures will provide your team members with a guide for the way they approach their own use of teams and their participation in decision making. Your actions will not only "shake the tree" around you but will also likely alter how the organization is run down through the ranks.

It's funny. I know CEOs who spend more time worrying about adding or deleting a member of their SMT than they spend on a 4,000-employee layoff. And it's not surprising. The executives on the SMT are the people you work with day to day. You need their continued commitment. And the perception of being demoted from the heights of Olympus can be hard to take.

Nevertheless it's time to take down the myth. If the behavioralists and organizational consultants haven't been able to fix your SMT, perhaps it's time to accept that it's a problem you have to fix yourself.

Expect some pushback. These changes go right to the heart of people's most sensitive issues of power, prestige, and places in the pecking order. There will be some wounded egos. Some people will complain or, as one CEO bluntly put it, "I had a few weeks of whining before things settled down."

You may have to weather a period of people knocking on your door seeking reassurance about their value to you and organization. But making tough calls and doing what's best for the organization is the life of the CEO. As always, explain your rationale clearly and repeatedly—and hold your ground. The storm will blow over quickly, and you'll have what you want.

And most of your people will soon see that they have what they want as well, and the others will either sulk or rise to the occasion.

Repurposing the SMT

Many clients begin to roll out the portfolio approach by rechartering existing teams, rationalizing standing committees, defining and populating initiative teams, and then parceling out relevant tasks among these groups. Although that may prove successful, I've always favored first re-anchoring the SMT in its new alignment-focused role, establishing a firm foundation on which to build the new structure.

Logic (and the order of the chapters of this book) might argue for starting with vision—creating a shared perspective about the company's environment and strategic direction. I recommend that you begin, instead, by having the SMT undertake the prioritization and integration of initiatives, through the types of conversations and mechanisms detailed in Chapter Eight. It's far better to get the SMT members up to their elbows in the far less abstract task of "bull's-eyeing" initiatives—prioritizing and integrating the handful of key strategic initiatives that they will be responsible for overseeing. Right away, the SMT will be performing one of its critical functions: allocating and managing the organization's strategic resources.

Because the SMT represents all parts of the organization, it is also ideally suited to help execute the next step in the implementation: influencing the design of the rest of the team and committee structure on the basis of strategic objectives and the key initiatives they drive. Some initiatives may already be owned by a well-defined initiative team; others may require the creation of a new initiative team or the merger of existing teams. Assuming initiative team oversight was left as an open issue when you announced the new portfolio structure, the SMT can now have a sense of ownership over the initiative teams and can see the importance of the SMT's continued investment in their success.

With your portfolio of teams clarified, the SMT launched in its expanded role, and the emergence of a culture of outcomes-focused management of teams, you will be well on the way to significant benefits: better decision support; less time wasted in meetings; more successful initiatives; a more efficient, agile, and aligned organization; and increased velocity in your business. Immediate benefits, like freeing people to meet less and get more work done, will create enthusiasm for the change. Medium-term benefits, like the energizing of the SMT in its more consequential role, will help build momentum. And long-term benefits, like fewer initiatives stalled and more initiatives succeeding, will sustain that momentum far into the future.

Who's in the Room?

None of what I'm suggesting here involves hiring a single psychologist, conducting any team-building exercises, or undertaking a personal transformation of the leader. Behavior in the organization will certainly change, but not because anyone's psyche has been massaged. Behavior will change because clarity has been established about structure, process, and roles—which is the essence of good management. That's where you should begin. Then if you still sense problems with your executive team or if you're not fully satisfied with what you're getting from them, by all means call in the shrinks to work with the group. But behavioralist solutions shouldn't be the first resort, because it's highly likely that whatever problems you perceive aren't rooted in psychology. They're rooted in suboptimal use of your team, or asking the team to do the impossible.

As you clarify and alter the structures, processes, and roles of all your teams, you will of course continue to consult with your close advisers and to make decisions in the way that best suits you. That remains unchanged. And I want to be absolutely clear about this: your job as CEO doesn't start with making decisions in a way that pleases other people (except, perhaps, your board). Your job is to make good decisions.

That's the real reason for paying close attention to who's in the room and what goes on there, because ultimately there is one room where all the activities in the other rooms converge—that place in your head where, alone, you decide.

Acknowledgments

It's said that only three things increase as they are shared: fire, knowledge, and love.

I've been the beneficiary of a great many people who took the time and effort to share their knowledge with me. And some of what I've learned as a result has ended up in the quotes, stories, and opinions expressed in this book.

A combination of limited space, a flawed memory, and the constraints of client confidentiality make it impossible for me to thank all these friends and mentors by name. But there are many people who have been tremendously helpful to me over the years, and I wanted to start with a collective thank-you to all of them before singling out a few: my professors at Tufts and Yale, including James Elliott, who taught me political theory; LaRue Hosmer, who taught me business policy; Sid Winter, who taught me about business models; Vic Vroom, who taught me about leadership; Martin Shubik, who taught me game theory; and especially the former dean of the Yale School of Management, Sharon Oster, who first taught me strategy. And, of course, my colleagues in the Blue Sky Club, who taught me the true value of a solid business case around the tables down at Mory's.

Management consulting is a craft, and my colleagues and mentors at The Boston Consulting Group, Gemini Consulting, and Accenture were the people who truly taught me my trade. The hundreds of partners and thousands of consultants who made these three firms great places to work and learn are far too numerous for me to mention all of them here, but in particular, I owe a great debt of gratitude to Bruce Henderson, Tony Miles, E. Y. Snowden, Shyam Gidumal, Mike Ericksen, Judy Hopelain, Fred Sturdivant, Larry Bennigson, Francis Gouillart, Jim Duffy, Gail Breslow, John Garabedian, Gary Getz, Peter Migliorato, Tom Wiseman, Ned Crosby, Bob Gray, Pierre Hessler, Juergen Schmidt, Volker Gerlach, John Kelly, Bret Bero, Charles Roussel, Bill Copacino, Bill Whitely, Dave Rey, Doug Ryckman, Yom Senegor, Charles Kalmbach, David Smith, Nick Palmer, and Steve Fowler. Others in my industry and the academic world, including Doug Stotz, Michael Treacy, Tom Stewart, Charlie Fine, and Joe Jacobson, have been great friends and generous sources of intellectual inspiration.

My current and former partners and colleagues at The Strategic Offsites Group have made the past decade the greatest in my professional career. Cary Greene, Andrew McIlwraith, Jon Hammer, Robin Lackey, Rebecca Maescher, Kathryn Gibson, Logan Chandler, and Josh Peck have all contributed to building a truly great firm, working tirelessly to do what we do better than anyone else in the world.

Lucia Gumbs, my executive assistant, is truly the glue that holds my professional life together. I can't thank her enough for keeping the trains running on time and for always keeping a cheerful disposition despite the occasional chaos that writing a book, running a firm, and serving clients can involve.

My mentors and colleagues during my two stints in industry at The Dial Corporation and Sears, Roebuck and Co. helped make me a far better consultant by teaching me to see the world through an executive's eyes. Ed Brennan, Jim Denny, Ed Liddy, Tom Wilson, Steve Shebik, Laura Dunne, Ivy Stern, Andy Patti, Mike Norman, Mike Cooper, Dan Lowe, and Paul Lustig are some of the people who showed me early in my career what being an executive entails.

A consultant without clients is, I suppose, unemployed. But far more than a source of livelihood, client relationships are what make consulting a great profession. Client confidentiality prevents me from thanking specific companies or people, but I am truly honored by the trust placed in me and my colleagues by our clients over the years.

Mine is the only name on the cover of this book, but an entire team helped make this project happen. I especially want to thank those executives who shared their time and opinions with me during the interview process, both those who permitted me to quote them by name and those who shared their opinions with me confidentially. You really made this book what it is.

I especially want to thank Tom Wilson, chairman and CEO of the Allstate Corporation, for providing his insights and perspective and for permitting me to share some of his experiences at Allstate in the case study in Chapter Five.

Steven Schragis generously shared his expertise in publishing and helped guide me along every step of the way. Eric Korman not only provided tremendous support and advice but gave the book its title. Jill Totenberg, at The Totenberg Group, has been an exceptional partner over the years, helping me to communicate a point of view about strategy and organizations. Jim Levine at The Levine Greenberg Literary Agency and Susan Williams at Jossey-Bass/Wiley have been wonderfully supportive partners to a first-time author.

Bruce Tucker is in a category by himself. Bruce has been my writer and editor for almost twenty years. Although his name does not appear on the cover, many of the words in this book are his. Bruce, I can't begin to thank you enough.

While the individuals I have already named, and many others, have shared their knowledge with me and contributed to my sharing it with you, I also want to thank those I love.

My mother, Bunny, late father, Lou, and brother, Norman, created a home where there was a constant environment of acceptance, support, love of reading, and encouragement to pursue wherever my curiosity took me. I couldn't have been luckier than to be born into a family like ours.

To my children, Jacob, Adam, Noah, and Rachael, the lights and joy of my life, I want to say that you've always had a dad who was away most of the week, and working in his home office many nights when he was home. But you always have a smile and a hug when I walk through the door. The four of you are children that Mom and I are truly proud of.

Iris, my wife, you are the most important person in my life. Raising four children with a weekend father is a difficult challenge for a mother. Your support is the only thing that has let me have both the career I dreamed of and the family I'd hoped for. You are the foundation of our home and the love of my life. You truly surpass them all.

The Author

Bob Frisch has twenty-nine years of experience designing and facilitating strategy offsites with executive teams and boards of companies ranging from Fortune 10 multinationals to family-held businesses. His work has been the subject of articles in publications ranging from *Fortune* to *CFO Magazine* to the *Johannesburg Business Report*. He is the author of three *Harvard Business Review* articles: "Who *Really* Makes the Big Decisions in Your Company?" (December 2011), "When Teams Can't Decide" (November 2008), and "Off-Sites That Work" (with Logan Chandler, June 2006). A magna cum laude graduate of Tufts, he earned his MBA degree at the Yale School of Management.

Bob founded his current firm, The Strategic Offsites Group, a decade ago. Previously, he held leadership roles in three of the world's most prominent consulting firms—Accenture, where he was a managing partner; Gemini Consulting, Europe's largest consultancy, where he headed the global practice in corporate vision and growth; and The Boston Consulting Group, where he was a founder of BCG's Los Angeles office.

In addition to his successful consulting career, Bob has twice temporarily taken on senior executive roles. He ran planning and business development for The Dial Corporation, going on to become the youngest division president of this Fortune 500 company. Five years later he led corporate strategy for Sears, Roebuck and Co., where he helped to guide what was at the time the largest voluntary restructuring in history.

Dangerous Company, a best-selling book on the consulting industry, says of Bob: "He has been there, small company and big, strategy and operations. He has lived much of his professional life on the road or in the corridors of power of huge institutions. In the game of business, he is equipped to be the perfect coach."

Bob lives in Newton Centre, Massachusetts, with his wife, Iris, and their children, Jacob, Adam, Noah, and Rachael.

Index